EETING MR KIM

Or How I Went to Korea and Learned to Love Kimchi

Jennifer Barclay

summersdale

08/06/09

MEETING MR KIM
Copyright © Jennifer Barclay 2008

Summersdale Publishers Ltd
46 West Street
Chichester
West Sussex
PO19 1RP
UK

www.summersdale.com

Maps by Rob Smith

Printed and bound in Great Britain

ISBN: 978-1-84024-676-6

ABOUT THE AUTHOR

Jennifer Barclay has written on travel, culture and books for *The Korea Herald*, *The Globe and Mail* and *The East* and is a regular contributor to the blog www.londonkoreanlinks.net. Co-editor of *AWOL: Tales for Travel-Inspired Minds*, she has lived in several countries and is now based in West Sussex.

'Errors of one sort and another there undoubtedly are in this account, but the truth is that something happened to me and that I have given as truthfully as I know how.'

Henry Miller, *The Colossus of Maroussi*

CONTENTS

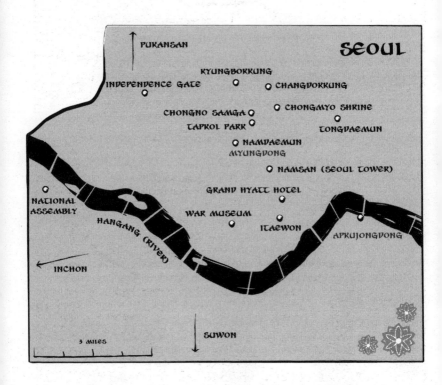

PROLOGUE

3 May 2006
Dear Jenny,
I received your email in surprise. I frequently think of
Songnisan and you whenever I see your pictures you sent
me. Thank you for your mail again. I feel that two days and
a night in 2000 will lead to our eternal friendship. Nowadays
I live in Seoul with my family. I am told that you plan to
write a book about Korea. I wish I could help you with your
writing. For now, I am determined that my getting touch
with you will last forever. If you should pay a visit to Seoul
again, I will have an opportunity to be proud of my country
through travelling with you.

Sincerely yours,

Wook

14 July 2007, New Malden, London

Mr Kim tells me Korean food is the most highly developed in the world. He is spending the day standing over a searingly hot barbecue cooking *galbi*, beef marinated in seventeen different ingredients. His white T-shirt somehow manages to remain immaculate, although he is slinging dripping steaks onto the grill all day.

'French food is seen as the best in the world. The French, they have one hundred and seventy different cuts of the cow, of beef. Koreans, we have more than two hundred. Close to three hundred.'

An impressive fact, although I wonder privately if it is a good thing to eat that many parts of a cow. The thinly sliced meat tastes sweet, however, and I'm impressed that young men like Mr Kim are spending their Saturday helping at the London Korean community's annual food festival. All the Korean restaurants come together in the expansive garden of a local pub to create a cultural gathering. I come prepared to eat lots.

I start off with *tokboki*, and the friendly lady whose table I share asks 'Are you OK with this spicy food?' It's pleasantly crunchy with carrot, cabbage and spring onion. The sun comes out and she goes to seek shade, leaving space for an older Indian couple who sit down to eat *bulgogi*, marinated beef and rice. We are watching the taekwondo demonstration – tiny kids breaking blocks of wood with their kicks and punches. My objective today is to expand my Korean culinary horizons, and I am lucky to be invited to join a group of Korean friends at a table where we can share mounds of food, giving me a chance to taste a range of dishes and learn about them in good company. We're in the shade of a tree and we have some drinks too. 'You know we Koreans have to keep eating side dishes in order to keep drinking!'

I trawl the food stalls and come back to the table with two new dishes. The first is *soondae*, slices of a dark sausage, griddle-fried with hot sauce and cabbage. Only when I put it on the table do I spot unmistakable slices of tripe lurking among the cabbage. My new friend TJ tells me it is good for the stomach and for energy! The *soondae* is squishy, with a chewy skin; someone says it's like haggis but there is none of the spice of haggis, and the texture is more like the French *boudin* or black pudding. The tripe stays on the plate. TJ is disappointed. 'It is better than snake!' No, I think I could eat snake. 'Better than dog!' he jokes.

My second experiment is *tongdwaeji*: slivers of spit-roasted pork, served with hot red garlicky sauce, slices of raw garlic and green hot chilli peppers, and – the really intriguing part – a spoonful of miniscule shrimp, each the size of a few grains of rice. The owner of the restaurant that supplied this today – whom I met a couple of weeks ago with his hands stuck in a bucket of wet cabbage, giving kimchi demonstrations – told me he and his chef hung this whole pig carcass on a spit, all sixty-nine kilos of it, last night so it could cook for seven hours, all the fat dripping away. Apparently the mini-shrimp are to aid digestion. The pork is lean and delicious, the prawns incredibly salty.

The traditional music finishes and the karaoke is now going strong beside our table. As friends come and go, getting up to see other friends or buy food, more drinks are spilled than I have ever seen at one table. On the grass, older ladies are dancing to 'YMCA'. A smartly dressed man sings 'My Way' and a young Korean woman with a surprisingly huge voice gets a standing ovation from the crowd. London has managed to provide weather that is almost summery – although it changes four times a day, like a woman, says TJ. The tripe stays on the table.

My love affair with Korea started in the year 2000, when the following story unfolds, and I finally finished writing it in 2007. While some aspects of life in the Republic of Korea will have changed by now, I have tried to make sense of my own experiences, which took place at a vital time in the country's evolution, by placing them in the context of Korean history and culture. In that way, I hope it will be a lasting tribute, and go some small way to enhancing an outsider's understanding of Korean culture through the adventures and misadventures of one bumbling westerner.

PART ONE: INTO THE UNKNOWN

*'When have I not been weary in winter time,
or indeed anywhere when settled?'*

Edward Lear

CHAPTER ONE:

PUTTING ON DRINKING BOOTS AND SPREADING MY WINGS

There had to be something wrong.

In the ratings of best places to live in the world, Toronto kept coming out top. Then why did I find myself crying when I flew back there after Christmas? Landing at Pearson Airport, I stood outside and saw only bland colours and concrete. As I took the bus downtown, a woman yelled into a mobile phone, enormous trucks barrelled past on the highway and the huge maple-leaf flag billowed in an icy January wind outside the Molson brewery, and I didn't want to be there. Even my favourite view of the skyscrapers from the lakeshore didn't make me happy.

I was renting an apartment on Fairview Boulevard, the top floor of a big old house in the east of the city. I'd just turned thirty and noticed my friends were beginning to buy houses. Perhaps living abroad kept me feeling like I didn't need to grow up. Now I wondered glumly whether deep down I didn't want to live in Toronto forever, and whether seven years was long enough to spend in a place you didn't want to stay in. It wasn't that I was particularly homesick for England, but – I sighed, putting my bags down and the kettle on – I was no longer sure if this road was leading where I wanted to go.

Stuck to the fridge door was a photo of the pretty village in green hills where I grew up and which we left when I was eighteen. I thought about how my mother was already bringing up two kids there by the time she was my age. I just had a mixed-up accent, a continual reminder that I was at home nowhere, and still didn't know what I wanted to make of my life.

I'd recently had such a run of rotten liaisons I was beginning to despair on that front. Not that I had any trouble meeting people, oh no. The previous summer there'd been someone utterly devoted, practical enough to build me bookshelves, rough around the edges but with quirky habits like playing the accordion, and his kids were delightful. But his surprise drug habit – well, I'd spent an exhausting few months trying to get the guy into rehab and out of my life. Others I met were as cold and brutal as a Canadian winter. Surprised how often I was getting hurt, I announced to my friend Patrick over a glass of red wine one evening,

'Maybe I should become a complete bitch.'

'No, babe,' he advised, adding what of course I already knew: 'You've just got to be yourself and wait for the right person to come along.' So at least I wasn't a complete bitch yet, according to Patrick anyway.

I'd come to Canada for rather arbitrary reasons. Shortly after university, at the end of a year teaching English in Greece, a chance meeting while swimming in the Mediterranean had led in a circuitous way to Canada and marriage. So much went wrong during that marriage it's hard to believe it only lasted a year and a half. But I'd decided to stay on in Toronto for a while, having finally found my way into a career – working with books and writers.

From admin assistant and general dogsbody, I was promoted year after year as the literary agency I worked for expanded. The youngest agent in town, I was surrounded by brilliant people, and a portfolio of press clippings on my clients was developing nicely. I had an assistant and a comfortable office – with a couch, no less, which my boss had had lifted by painstaking means to my third-floor coop in the stylish house the agency occupied. But I was surely, irresistibly, feeling a seven-year itch. With little time for anything but work, I'd started to hate fancy restaurants and was frankly tired of responsibility, of bitchiness, of pushing myself hard all the time. I felt like I was faking – faking that I knew what I was doing, faking the veneer – maybe I wasn't posh enough for this posh job. A certain hysterical cynicism gripped me one day when I discovered I could do most of my job hungover in bed, wearing pyjamas with a phone against my ear.

Building up a client list, always on the brink of some breakthrough, I hadn't taken more than a week's holiday for years. I couldn't go on. I saw the possibility of becoming bitter and twisted, or at least terminally unhappy, unless I made a change. I needed to get away from business, from being professional. I needed to play. So I did the only reasonable thing. I prepared to quit my job and go travelling.

And then, at the end of January, I quite unexpectedly found myself in the back of a cab snogging an Irishman nine years my junior.

I had met Gavin a few months earlier in my local Irish pub, where he was working as a bartender after dropping out of university to be a drummer in a band. He was tall with short reddish hair and, being a musician, a little unshaven square under his bottom lip called a soul patch. He had a sharp mind and a powerful ability to make me laugh, and together we were able to recite entire scenes from the telly programme *The Young Ones*, to the bafflement of everyone around. We'd got to know one another as friends, both seeing other people. But as January ended and those relationships foundered, we were both suddenly single. And to be fair, I didn't realise quite how young he was at the time.

His band, Good Vibes, was playing at a bar downtown and recording a video for their agent. Although I had a miserable cold, a mutual friend emailed me: 'Get your drinking boots on – it's the boy's birthday.' Gav was surprised to see his pals out in force – and rather humiliated, for the video had to be shot in stage costume. Good Vibes, I knew, was a funk and R'n'B cover band, but he'd kept quiet about the costumes. Since the agent was hunting down an international contract, there would be no half measures. Thus it was that I saw him sheepishly sporting an electric-blue sequined shirt and white shiny trousers on the night we began to realise a relationship between us might be possible. Perspicaciously, he changed his clothes after the show. In the taxi back to our neighbourhood at the end of his twenty-second birthday, we were suddenly kissing, and the idea of going out with a bartender/musician nine years younger than me didn't seem all that silly... As they say, how can it be wrong, when it feels so right?

February and March went beautifully. We laughed, we danced; we had dinners of sparkling Banrock Station and deliveries from Sushi Delight while sitting cross-legged on the bed. Meanwhile, I worked as hard as I could, closed deals and put money away for my travels. I prepared for the task, after the London Book Fair, of informing all my clients I would be leaving that spring, and tried to orchestrate a few last deals; I had a satisfying coup for one of my favourite authors, and it felt like a good note to leave on. My boss was supportive of the decision to 'spread my wings', and I knew the clients I liked would understand my decision. They nicely also said they'd miss me. The others – well, sod them. People said I was doing something brave (read: stupid), but for my own sanity it felt absolutely right to be taking a break. I longed for the date of impending freedom, even though I still hadn't got around to booking a ticket anywhere.

Gav's band played gigs around the city and the suburbs, and many a late night I stood about while they loaded equipment into vans in freezing parking lots, acquainting myself with the glamour of the music business. Funk wasn't exactly Gav's favourite music – he was a rock fan, with interests ranging from King Crimson to Oasis to Nick Cave; he'd bravely played me the *Murder Ballads* the first time I stayed at his place. Nor were sequins and PVC his number one fashion choice, but as a drummer he liked to get people dancing, and there was a certain cachet for a white guy in being the main rhythm section in an otherwise black funk band. One of their songs was, appropriately enough, 'Play That Funky Music, White Boy'. Besides, the real reason he'd joined Good Vibes was his dream to be a professional musician and see the world at the same time. We were on our way to the video store one evening when he excitedly told me the news:

'We've got a contract to play in Asia. Three months in the club of the Seoul Grand Hyatt.'

Beneath my happy congratulations there was an awful sinking feeling. I'd just found a lovely man, and now he was going to the other side of the world. Then again, so was I. I just hadn't decided exactly where yet.

Although most people have a wish list of places to go, I've always been perversely attracted to travelling in places I know nothing about. I love the serendipitous trip, the chance to travel somewhere I've never even contemplated going before. A few days later, I casually aired the idea that since I was going travelling anyway, maybe we could go to Korea together.

It turned out he'd been thinking the same. In Seoul, he would be busy playing in the band, so I'd have plenty of time for the solo exploring I liked – but we wouldn't have to be apart for months. We both agreed that being apart for months was not conducive to a lasting relationship, not for us. I'd failed at it before. It seemed absurd not to give this a try, when we got along pretty well, give or take some late-night arguments. It would be an adventure, and neither of us would mind being alone there if it didn't work out. Gav was due to fly out at the start of May with the rest of the band and a mound of drumming gear. Ignoring the gentle ribbing from friends about running away with my rock musician toy boy, I booked a ticket that would allow me to work out my notice and get me to Seoul at the end of May.

My taste for travelling to lesser-known places comes partly from my dad's family, who visited our Lancashire village from such exotic places as Bermuda and Botswana when I was an impressionable girl. It's also a reaction against 'must-see' travel: top ten places to go, sights not to miss, how many stars does this experience get? The magic of wandering, finding unlooked-for pleasures, uncovering places for yourself: I'd much rather experience an unknown place myself than queue up with thousands of others to see the famous one. Unexpected beauty means so much more; you see it with your own eyes.

Soon, thirty-two games of World Cup football would be played there, but for now, all most people could think of when you said 'Korea' was the Korean War, that old television programme *M*A*S*H*, and cheap manufactured electronics. Having never seen *M*A*S*H*, and being useless at modern history, I felt completely in the dark.

I started to read up. The Korean peninsula, stuck halfway between China and Japan, has been divided into two countries for over fifty years since the Korean War. The capital of South Korea, Seoul, is on roughly the same latitude as Beijing or Tokyo, Spain or Greece. The country has cold, dry winters and hot, wet summers. You didn't need a lot of inoculations to visit (just one, against Japanese encephalitis, not considered a big risk). South Korea, or the Republic of Korea, the ROK, has a population of forty-five million – close to that of England, though the landmass is smaller, nearer the size of Portugal. As long as North Korea didn't attack, a very remote possibility, South Korea was deemed a safe country for tourists. It had beaches and mountains – those details appealled. After enduring yet another long and brutal Toronto winter, I could handle some lounging on beaches and wandering in mountains. I pictured myself becoming tanned and slim, letting my nails grow, relaxing and absorbing the local culture effortlessly.

The brother of an ex-boyfriend and his fiancée, who had taught English in Seoul a few years earlier, agreed to meet me in a local bar. They mentioned getting mildew on their clothes during rainy season, but otherwise they were fairly positive, though they didn't seem to have seen much of the country beyond the capital and couldn't tell me much. Anyway, I wanted to be surprised by Korea.

I sublet the apartment on Fairview Boulevard for the next six months, finding a couple who loved it instantly the way I had, and whom I trusted enough that I could leave my belongings in one of the huge unlockable cupboards that stretched into the roof. With great excitement I said goodbye to the dirty streets, where blackened snowbanks – the mounds of snow that accumulate on pavements throughout the winter in the city – were finally melting and turning to dust. I said goodbye to the dull, brown post-winter grass and, for rather arbitrary reasons, made a journey to Seoul, Korea.

CHAPTER TWO:

SPECIAL TOURISM ZONE

In the Korean War between 1950 and 1953, 47,000 Korean and 37,000 United Nations troops lost their lives in South Korea, and more than a million in the North, while some accounts say as many as three million Korean civilians also died. The UN troops were mostly Americans, but also British, Africans, Europeans, Asians, South Americans and Australians. Images of those years show frozen mud, tanks, bomb craters, death. Seoul had to be completely rebuilt after the uneasy ceasefire that ended the fighting in 1953. North Korean guerrillas were still infiltrating Seoul in the late sixties, and there were many scares of invasions by land and submarine – even from underground, as tunnels had been discovered burrowing under the border, wide enough for tanks.

The main US army base, built to protect the South from invasion by the North, is in Seoul, near Itaewon at Yongsan – where, at *the start of the twentieth century, the Japanese invading army was based. It seems strange to me to have such a big US army presence in the middle of the city, a garrison of 630 acres, but then North and South Korea are still at war.*

The bar was dark and crowded as Good Vibes rocked the room with their high-energy funk. At tables glinting with whisky bottles, respectable Asian businessmen in grey suits swept their arms through the air as they swayed vaguely to the beat, eyes closed and ties loosened. A young executive leapt around the dance floor, wiggling his hips, his jacket swinging from one hand and, from the other, the belt he'd somehow removed. The businessmen's wives, delicate ladies in silk with immaculate hair, boogied gracefully to 'Brick House'.

After a very long day flying, my first afternoon in Seoul had been a blur. I'd been on a plane full of short middle-aged Asians I assumed to be Koreans, all wearing casual clothes and washable beige hats. My man met me at Kimpo International Airport with a red rose and whisked me into town in a taxi, past blockish high-rises, the imposing, monolithic National Assembly building, and general big city chaos. It was a greyish day, but we giggled at being together again.

The Grand Hyatt Hotel was a prominent slab of smoky mirrored glass on a big hill called Namsan. I had a quick tour: an enormous air-conditioned lobby lined with chestnut-stained wood and Cartier and Rolex boutiques, cathedral-sized windows looking down over lush gardens and beyond them a mass of urban conrete, pale grey in hazy sunlight. Someone was playing a piano in the lounge.

'This is where I come to have a coffee and read the paper sometimes,' said Gav. He'd raved about the place on the phone. 'There's a couple of Polish girls who play violin and flute in the afternoons. Come on, I'll show you JJ's.' He took me to the downstairs level to see the nightclub, which was empty except for a few staff polishing glasses for the evening. We didn't have much time to look around as Gav had to get ready for work.

The band had shared hotel rooms for the first week, then moved out to apartments. We had one to ourselves for now, a five-minute walk away in a small, modern flat-roofed block, decorated blandly with lino floors and plastic furniture. There was a place to leave your shoes by the door before you stepped up onto the raised floor, but otherwise it was furnished in western style: kitchen, living room, bedrooms, bathroom with a shower. I pulled crumpled clothes, a dozen books and the laptop computer from my backpack and got dressed to go back to the Hyatt and see the show.

Posh hotels – the Hyatt was classed as 'Super Deluxe' – really weren't my natural environment. I'd rather have the surprise of freshly shucked oysters from a grubby bucket on the beach than sit in the hippest spa hotel and be served them on a designer plate. I preferred a bit of edge; my latest going-out outfit back in Toronto had included black bovver boots and a second-hand fireman's greatcoat. But for my first night at the Hyatt to see the show I managed jeans and platform sandals and a skimpy top.

JJ Mahoney's looked plush and tasteful by night, with leather upholstery lining the walls and subdued lighting. I stood swaying my hips tentatively, clutching my bottle of beer. It was the same routine of cover songs they'd been practising for the last few months, so I knew it well. Dividing the stage from the audience was a semi-circular bar attended by efficient, slick waiters. I'd got to know the band: Dean the lead guitarist and band leader with a drooping Mexican moustache and long ponytail and lots of gold necklaces; Vinny the percussionist with a shaved head and wraparound black sunglasses; Leroy the male singer with a habit of saying 'yeah yeah yeah' and grinning constantly; Barry the quiet, corpulent, older bass player; and Shauna the young, slim, female singer with a winning smile. They played funk, soul and R'n'B, with a few of the current vacuous pop numbers by Cher and Britney thrown in. Sneer as I might, they made you want to dance.

'Hello Seoul Korea! Allriiiight!'

Between songs, Dean announced Good Vibes was 'all the way from Canada' and excited screams were offered in response. The drummer, thrashing away at the back of the stage, dropped his serious face for a moment to flash me the hint of a smile. For Gav, drumsticks functioned like mere extensions of the fingers; as he talked to you, he flicked them and spun them and created little drum rolls on the back of the couch. Being on stage was like a drug in his veins. Signing autographs later didn't hurt. So this was the rock and roll lifestyle in North East Asia. Well, not really, but it was close. They weren't big in Japan, they weren't big in Korea, but they were big in JJ Mahoney's Bar.

27

For a few weeks now, they had been playing western pop six nights a week to entertain the city's elite. The nightclubs of the big hotels in Seoul were prestigious, and the Grand Hyatt was top dog. It was the hotel for oil tycoons, foreign ministers, magnates like Bill Gates and heads of state like Bill Clinton. A bottle of Johnny Walker in JJ's cost around US$500, and there were several evident on the tables. The small bottle of local OB beer I was nursing had set me back US$10, and if you wanted Heineken it was US$15. It was for this sort of ambiance the band had to wear the sparkly suits. On the plus side, it was an enviable contract for them: three months being paid a regular wage in US dollars, with free accommodation. Gav was now a professional musician, and he was travelling. Play that funky music, white boy.

As they launched into a soulful number and Leroy crooned 'Let's get it on', I made my way to the bar to invest in another small bottle of beer. A Korean man in a sweater and thick Coke-bottle glasses, who'd been coming to see the band regularly, confessed to me his favourite musician of all time was 'Otis Reeding'. Tough guys in black suits sat at the bar behind tall glasses of fruity cocktails with umbrellas, ogling Shauna. 'I've seen these guys pay the bartender a tip of US$200 just to keep their seat for the night,' Gav had said. Beside European businessmen and hulking American army officers sat sleek Korean women with long black hair; in the toilets, however, they turned into skinny girls who smoked nervously, stared into mirrors, and spat on the floor.

A rift had developed already in the band because Gav hadn't joined the others in sampling the local girls before I arrived. 'It's just not my bag, man,' said Gav, since most of those offering themselves up were actually prostitutes. A friend of his back home, who spent his holidays in the seedier parts of Malaysia, had said Gav was mad taking a girlfriend along to Asia. Ugh, that creepy nudge-nudge attitude among guys when it comes to Asian girls, Swedish girls, French girls. And what is it about Kylie Minogue that all men like? What?!

When the show ended around 2 a.m., Gav and I jumped into a taxi and headed a short distance down the hill to Itaewon, the district that grew up around the US army base to cater for soldiers' needs. This was a bit more interesting. In the area affectionately known as Hooker Hill, we wandered down streets lined with 'Gentlemen's Entertainment' clubs like Fun Girls Country Club and Kiss in the Dark, advertising in lurid neon such unthinkable delights of the flesh as 'Fine Drinks!', 'Beautiful Women!' and – avert your eyes, not for the faint-hearted – 'Darts!' The sleaze was pervasive but mild, and there were food stalls everywhere for the undiscriminating late-night partier: fried fish, fried pancakes, sausage-shaped white rice cakes in hot red sauce, potatoes-on-a-stick. Standing in the stickily humid night, we ate chicken skewers slathered with barbecue sauce.

Back on the main street we walked to Hollywood, one of a handful of dance clubs open all night on the upper floor of a nondescript building, and breezed in like VIPs for free because of Gav's minor celebrity status. 'Get this,' said Gav. 'Last week we were partying with the Red Hot Chilli Peppers. They love us here.' Hollywood was an unsophisticated but lively place frequented by foreigners, visiting or resident, and young Koreans, mostly women.

When Gav said he'd had a hard time shaking off a Korean girl one night, I tried not to be jealous.

At Hollywood we ran into half of a young Australian band who had a contract playing at the Hard Rock Cafe. Gav had met them a couple of weeks earlier, and now he offered to buy the bass player a beer. 'What about a jug, man?' Adam retorted. Gav, beaming, came back from the bar loaded with glasses and a frosted pitcher of beer. It was easy to dance the rest of the night away. At dawn, the music stopped and the curtains were opened and everyone staggered into the smoggy, faintly fetid streets, donning sunglasses against the bright grey morning. As we took a cab back up the hill, away from this little international enclave, I saw groups of Korean men squatting on their haunches to chat at the roadside, beside enormous piles of garlic that looked like snowbanks.

Next day we walked down the hill into Itaewon again for an expensive and awful breakfast of weak coffee and tasteless toast. Seedy Itaewon had been designated the 'Special Tourism Zone' of the city. In the harsh light of day, this seemed designed to put tourists off Seoul. The main street had been completely dug up for the construction of a new subway line, leaving a big brown crater and muddy, chaotic walkways on either side. Interspersed with bars and the occasional restaurant, dusty little shops and stalls crowded the pavements, all selling the same knock-off Prada T-shirts, Gucci belts, Louis Vuitton luggage and Rolex watches, as well as custom-made suits and onyx chess sets. Maybe Special Tourism was simply a euphemism for what went on in the Gentlemen's Entertainment Clubs?

On the subject of Special Tourism Zones, it was now possible for non-Koreans to take an organised trip to the DMZ, the DeMilitarized Zone and site of the armistice negotiations of 1953, some way north of Seoul. This was the borderland that divided North and South, the sloping line that was drawn across Korea, heavily defended on either side of the four kilometres of no-man's-land. You had to dress appropriately to visit – no jeans, no long hair for men, no short dresses for women, and no military clothing unless part of a prescribed uniform. The day trip included a military escort to Freedom House to glimpse North Korea, well known as the most closed society in the world. In 1976, two US servicemen were hacked to death by North Koreans at the DMZ. The idea of going to see this as a tourist seemed macabre to me.

The no-man's-land, a swathe of land on either side of the Demarcation Line that crosses the Korean peninsula from the East Sea to the Yellow Sea, had been largely untouched by humans for half a century and had now inadvertently become a wildlife sanctuary: somehow a sign of hope, of rebirth. It remained the principal site of the peace dialogues. In a couple of weeks, fifty years after the outbreak of the war in June 1950, the first-ever peace summit between the leaders of North and South Korea, Chairman Kim Jong-il and President Kim Dae-jung, was about to take place in the North's capital, Pyongyang.

The world is understandably fascinated by North Korea. It became a communist country in 1948 and is 'the secret state'. It lends itself to sinister speculation, 'chilling photographs' on CNN, and makes a perfect enemy for James Bond or *Spooks*. Its frightening nuclear programme is in the hands of a dictator with a bouffant haircut and aging Elvis look.

Kim Il-sung, his father, shaped North Korea over an astonishing forty-eight-year reign, and was named 'eternal president' a few years after his death in 1997. Chairman Kim Jong-il inherited the state just as all first sons inherit their father's business in Korean culture. Since then he has run a Stalinist regime, without basic human rights such as freedom of speech or freedom to leave. Radios receive only one official station, allowing its citizens no real understanding of the outside world. The official line given by its leaders is that North Korea is a paradise of equality with no need for outside links; a nation that works together as happily as it sings and dances together in the massive performances it likes to show the world. This image was shattered after the truth came out about years of horrific famine, which killed as much as ten per cent of the population. Dissidents occasionally smuggle out pictures that tell the truth. Stories have emerged of concentration camps for political prisoners, public executions of those trying to escape, homeless children, people lying dead in the streets of hunger and cold. The camps must have been so effective that in the 1980s Zimbabwean dictator Robert Mugabe invited North Koreans to Zimbabwe to torture and kill 'dissidents' in his own detention centres.

Kang Chol-hwan, in his book *The Aquariums of Pyongyang*, described how he spent ten years of his childhood in a North Korean gulag. For no real reason, his whole family was consigned to slave labour, near starvation and imprisonment. The account tells of a corrupt society where bribes are the only way to survive; of people reduced to eating grass, children's skin rotting from infection, and of the author's frustration, after he escaped to South Korea in 1992, on meeting students who argued in favour of communism.

It is North Korea that preoccupies the media, naturally, and it is important that we understand what is going on there – but I was here to get to know the South. It's ironic that the world knows more about the secret state of North Korea than its free, open counterpart to the south. Little South Korea has always been overshadowed by China the giant to the west, Japan the strong, once-imperial power to the east, the strange communist regime of North Korea, and Russia to the north of that. What a shame South Korea is mostly known for its war, when in fact it's such a peaceful nation, never having invaded another country. It was a troubled place for many years, and the only people who tended to come here apart from the US soldiers and the businessmen were English language teachers, usually recent graduates from North America here to pay off their crippling student loans; none of them had much time to travel around.

There weren't many tourists at all here, it seemed. In this Special Tourism Zone of Itaewon, however, there was a little Tourist Information kiosk, and I picked up a copy of a brand-new government magazine in English called *Welcome to Korea*, the very first issue. It suggested places to see in Korea that were unrelated in any way to the war: firefly festivals, mud bath festivals, and ancient royal music performed once a year, classed as 'Intangible Cultural Property Number One'. It was this traditional culture I wanted to see. In the Korean national foundation myth, founder Tan-gun's mother was a bear who became a woman by eating twenty cloves of garlic and a bundle of mugwort and staying out of sunlight for twenty-one days. Who knew?

We stopped at a little roadside stall selling cheap jewellery, and bought a couple of plain silver rings. Partly for practical reasons, we decided to wear them on our wedding ring fingers; in this very foreign place, with its residual seediness, it might be easier to pretend we were married. It was also a romantic gesture, because we'd actually made it here together.

CHAPTER THREE:

THE NOODLES AND THE SCISSORS

Although today Korea is politically divided, Koreans have been Korean for thousands of years. When I think about my white British background, it's probably a mixture of various invaders, ancient Briton with Germanic Saxon, Roman, Viking Scandinavian and Norman French; there's also some Irish in me, and my grandfather came from Hungary. Koreans have been dominated by Chinese, by Mongols and by Japanese, and have lived with Americans for half a century; they have taken elements of other cultures and adapted them into Korean culture; but within Korea there has been hardly any intermarriage with other nationalities and the gene pool has essentially remained Korean.

Korea's relationship with Japan has been a difficult one. In the very south, the two countries are only 200 kilometres apart. Around AD400, Japanese raids on Korea resulted in the establishment of a small colony of Japanese on the Korean peninsula, followed by communities of Koreans settling in Japan. The Koreans, better educated at the time, passed on to the Japanese the Chinese script and skills such as metalwork and silkworm culture. According to Richard Storry's A History of Modern Japan, 'their contribution to the cultural development of Japan can hardly be overestimated'.

Then in 1592, an ugly, low-born and hugely ambitious Japanese general named Toyotomi Hideyoshi set out to conquer China via Korea. When the king of Korea refused passage, 200,000 Japanese troops stormed Pusan in the south and fought their way north via Seoul and Pyongyang to China. They were repelled by a combination of Chinese troops and the successes at sea of a Korean admiral named Yi Sun-shin; this was the brilliant man who invented the 'turtle-boat', a ship protected by a shell-like roof of iron. Hideyoshi returned in 1597, and inflicted much bloody fighting on Korea before both he and Yi died a year later, ending the conflict. The misery imposed on the Korean people through the Japanese army's cruelties, accompanied by famine and disease, left what Storry calls 'a legacy of hatred'.

So three hundred years later, when the Japanese wanted to open relations again with Korea – whose usefulness as a pawn in the war games of her larger neighbours was by then glaringly apparent – they were rudely rebuffed. But as tensions between Japan and Russia increased, an Anglo-Japanese alliance gave Britain's endorsement as Japan moved in to take over Korea. In 1904, Korea was forced to accept Japanese financial and diplomatic advisers. A year later, the king of Korea was persuaded to give control of foreign affairs to a Japanese resident-general. Gradually powers were eroded, the king *abdicated, and a Korean assassination of a Japanese general gave Japan an excuse to annex Korea in 1910.*

Good Vibes performed nightly from 9 p.m. to 2 a.m., so Gav slept until lunchtime and liked to rest before the show. But in the afternoons or on Sundays, his day off, we could take a taxi from the Hyatt and go exploring. Taxis were reasonably cheap, though spirits could be dampened by the mad traffic jams which left you sitting in the motionless cab, watching the meter. Today we drove around Namsan towards the heart of the city, passing Namdaemun.

Seoul has been inhabited for about six thousand years, since Neolithic times, and has been the capital for more than six hundred years. Namdaemun, the Great South Gate of the old city walls with an arched passageway for the king to pass through, had two huge black tiled roofs layered one above the other. Built in 1398 and then rebuilt in 1448, it somehow survived the Korean War that destroyed most of Seoul, and now held the noble title of Tangible National Treasure Number One – but was overlooked by concrete and glass high-rises and surrounded by a roundabout with several lanes of speeding traffic, so crazy you had to cross via subway passages. Home to nearly eleven million people, Seoul has almost a quarter of the entire population of South Korea. Smog and dust hang in the air, amid grids of utilitarian commercial office blocks.

We passed what looked like a Korean wedding party outside a restaurant. The women were dressed in traditional clothes, or *hanbok* – dresses of fine muslin fabrics in bright pinks and yellows with red trim, crossing the chest to make a 'V' at the neck, with a very high waist, wide sleeves and billowing skirts – with their black, straight hair pulled back into neat ponytails. As we swept up an eight-lane street, steep, jagged hills appeared in the near distance, bluish-green through a slight haze. Kyungbok Palace stood breathtakingly beautiful against that backdrop. Its heavy sloping wooden roofs curled skyward at the ends.

The taxi dropped us outside. Inside the gates, in a wide courtyard, cute Korean kids dressed smartly in jeans and trainers played around a temporary art installation of chrome spheres, which reflected the old architecture in the sparkling sunlight. The palace itself, so completely different from huge rectangular European stone palaces, was a series of wooden buildings, painted with flowers and dragons, around peaceful courtyards with trees and ponds. On the gables of the roofs, heavily laden with black tiles, stood the black figures of animal spirits. The wooden shutters were painted in delicate pinks and reds and greens, trellises rendered in different shades, lines accentuated here and there; an infinite attention given to how forms complemented each other, how a doorway led to another. Handmade Korean paper or *hanji* was used in windows because it kept out the humidity in the summer, and let through light from the sun and the moon. Built in the fifteenth century, Kyungbokkung had been destroyed many times by Japanese and other invaders over the centuries, and repeatedly rebuilt. After last being razed to the ground by the Japanese in the early twentieth century, Kyungbokkung was finally restored in the 1970s to its former grace, painstakingly reconstructed, and now stood as an island of serenity and a symbol of national pride.

On that sunny Sunday, Korean families were picnicking on the fringes of the palace grounds on raised wooden platforms with thatched roofs. We hadn't brought a picnic and the area around the palace, Kwanghwamun, was a highly gentrified district for ministries and cultural centres and the president's house – but on the other side of the street we found a proletarian little cafe. Pointing to a sign on the window, we ordered *kimchi tchigae* (pronounced 'chi-geh'), which we'd read was a spicy stew. Our Korean language skills being strictly rudimentary, we weren't too surprised when what came instead was a tray of dishes of tofu, green beans, yellow discs of pickled radish and tiny fried fish. Delighted by all these new flavours, we tucked in and washed it all down with a couple of beers. Just as we were getting ready to pay the bill, out came the *kimchi tchigae*: an enormous steaming vat of spicy soup, garlicky with chunks of tofu and sliced meat and lots of Chinese cabbage; accompanied by covered metals bowls of steamed rice. The rest had been hors d'oeuvres.

Seoul was overflowing with wonderful food, I soon discovered, and eating was taken seriously. People picnicked everywhere, setting out mats at the side of the road, even between parked cars. Delivery men zipped up the pavements on motorbikes, carrying dinner in steel cases; women delivered lunch on foot, trays carrying several different dishes balanced on their heads. In 'soju tents', makeshift places set up with orange tarpaulins in the street, people ate and drank all night; these places were frowned upon because they didn't conform to the government's vision of modern Korea, but they persisted nonetheless.

I had arrived entirely ignorant of Korean food; it was a completely unknown taste. Unlike many Asian flavours I was familiar with – Chinese, Indian, Thai, Vietnamese, Japanese – Korean had never penetrated my world. In Toronto, I used to be baffled by the stretch of Bloor Street between Bathurst and Christie known as Little Korea, where the signs were all in a strange script, all boxes and circles and sticks.

Who knew that learning this alphabet would be the easy part? It was developed by King Sejong in the fifteenth century using a scientific but simple system, which enabled ordinary people to write in their own language. Unchanged since then, *hangul* was indeed all boxes and circles and sticks; but they were easy to make sense of once you learned the sounds, based on phonetics. There were fourteen consonants and ten vowels, which joined in twos and threes to form syllables. I enjoyed learning new languages and this one had some logic to it. My notebook was already full of words I was learning assiduously, though I hadn't tried them out much except on the little old man who ran a tiny stall on our hill, where I started buying cartons of fruit juice and milk. I'd been somewhat flummoxed to learn that the numbers one to five varied depending on the kind of object you were counting – Chinese numbers for minutes and Korean for hours, either for days – but I assumed all would eventually become clear once I started talking to more people. I'd mastered *olmayeyo*, 'how much', and 'thank you', *kamsamnida* (short for *kamsa hamnida*).

Gav provided after-show club sandwiches from the Hyatt, and occasionally a meal in the hotel restaurant, international and expensive but outstanding. I started exploring the neighbourhood shops for everyday food, but at first resorted to buying the same few items I recognised: Cornflakes, fluffy white bread, tins of tuna and squeezy-bottle mayonnaise. Even something that looked reassuringly familiar could have a weird taste, such as a carton of tomato juice that turned out to be heavily sweetened. I tried buying some fresh noodles, but they just ended up tasting of flour as I had no idea what to buy to go with them. Where to begin? I would have to look around and watch what other people were buying. A market seemed a good place to start, so I dragged Gav along.

Namdaemun Market was one of Seoul's two main markets, both the size of small villages. Down one lane after another, stall after stall had different types of dried, edible seaweed and huge jars of giant ginseng roots with thick torsos and twisting tendrils suspended in red liquid, the root Koreans have cultivated for many centuries to improve health and energy. The market was also bursting with fresh produce: eels writhing in buckets, whole pigs' heads and feet proudly displayed, and live, fat greenish-brown sea cucumbers in tanks. Or were they sea slugs? I'd never thought much about either before. People sat at the stalls and ate them freshly plucked from the tank. These were foodstuffs I was probably never going to stomach.

There were also tables filled with knives, jungle hammocks, dark green blankets, camouflage trousers and night-vision binoculars. Evidently a great deal of army gear made its way into the markets. Other tables were heaped with checked shirts, chinos, and those round canvas hats with flat tops and narrow brims, distinctive pieces of Korean casual wear. Amid piles of made-in-Korea clothes, lots of western labels were in evidence and price tags showing high prices in pounds and euros that bore no relation to the handwritten signs in Korean won.

Bargaining was the order of the day, and Gav enjoyed that part. *Olmayeyo*? They got out a calculator and showed you the price; and you said *anyo* (short for *aniyo*), no, and they passed you the calculator so you could put in a counter-bid, back and forth until the price was right and you could say *nae*, yes. I got myself a khaki army T-shirt for 2,000 won and a pair of shorts with handy side-pockets for 10,000 won, 1,000 won being roughly equivalent to a US dollar. We found a couple of cheap army sleeping bags that might come in useful.

Namdaemun Market also sold a lot of knock-off watches, and Gav spent ages looking at them. In one dimly lit shop, its shelves crammed with boxes and parts, watches arrayed everywhere, we were baffled to find one with 'Gavin' written on the face. Naturally, we had to buy it. As we agreed on the fair price, the two men running the shop invited us to toast the purchase with a beer. From under the counter appeared some plastic cups and two large bottles that were shared out liberally. The shopkeepers were brothers, perhaps: each had faint eyebrows that curved in crescents above thin eyes, a squat nose and a square chin. As we sipped and smiled, they looked approvingly at Gav, admiringly even, and finally confessed they thought my man very 'hana-sum' because of his prominent nose and hairy arms. They smiled and praised his 'funny little beard'. Gav blushed slightly, but with his big blue eyes, bronze hair and his mustard-yellow short-sleeved shirt – which now showed off hefty biceps, thanks to all the drumming – he did indeed look hana-sum.

The simple way to learn about Korean food was to start sampling it in restaurants, you'd have thought. And yet, oddly enough, it wasn't that simple. Seoul wasn't the paradise of sushi bars we'd imagined it might be; we hadn't seen anything like a sushi bar in fact. We had tried one 'traditional Korean restaurant' in Itaewon, and ended up with a gritty, dirty-brown soup with a couple of whole dead fish in it. It wasn't clear what we should be looking for. There was also that gruesome fact that Koreans were known to eat dog meat; what if we ordered dog by mistake?

I decided to take the plunge one evening. Where we lived, on the lower slopes of Namsan between Itaewonno or Itaewon Street and the Hyatt, was a fairly ordinary neighbourhood, a jumble of modern, red brick, flat-roofed houses and small apartment buildings, with little shops and the occasional restaurant. There were no menus outside the restaurants, so I had no idea what it would cost or what they would serve, but halfway up the hill was a plain-looking place that appeared inexpensive.

The waitress couldn't understand what I wanted at first. What, her expression seemed to ask, is this foreign person doing here? I persevered. It couldn't be that much of a problem – I was a customer after all. I smiled, then gingerly removed my lace-up black trainers and left them by the door, stepping up onto the raised floor of the eating area in my socks, as you were supposed to. So far so good. It was quiet in the restaurant. I picked a table and sat down cross-legged on the floor, trying to look confident, trying to – ahem – blend in. I sit cross-legged on the floor a lot at home, so that part was easy.

The waitress came over to take my order. I realised there were no menus at all. I looked around. Maybe the handwritten sign on the wall was the menu, but I couldn't read it. Thankfully, the one or two other customers included a Korean businessman dressed in a suit, who spoke English fluently.

'Can I help you?' he asked.

'Thank you. I'm just not sure what to order. Can you recommend something?'

'I see! Well, yes, let me see… Do you like noodles? Yes, well, perhaps you should try *mool naengmyun*. It is a special summer dish of noodles.'

'Thank you! That sounds great.' I was relieved. 'Um, could you tell them that's what I would like?'

He did, adding, 'I'm not sure if you're going to like it, but it is good!' Then he went back to his own meal and his newspaper.

As I waited for it to come, I felt pleased to be sitting cross-legged at a table in Seoul. I've always found travel to be the best way of learning about the world, I thought to myself. When I'd first been given an opportunity to visit Guyana, for example, I barely knew where it was. But I'd learned so much from that trip, including some history of my own culture. I'd never been good at learning history or geography from textbooks – all those dates and facts slide instantly from my brain – and I'd always had a bad habit of avoiding newspapers, because they can be so depressing. But here I was, learning about Korea first-hand. How pride comes before a fall.

My *mool naengmyun*, which arrived in a large steel bowl, turned out to be a chilled clear broth with a clump of translucent grey vermicelli in the middle, with half a hard-boiled egg and a tiny bit of shredded vegetable stuck on top. *Hmmm*, I thought, underwhelmed. A squeezy bottle of red sauce came with it, and metal chopsticks and a flattish spoon. Then the waitress brought a very large pair of scissors, and I knew I was way out of my depth.

I tentatively picked up the metal chopsticks and plunged them into the clumped mass of noodles. But the noodles stuck together and had the elasticity of bungee cords. There was no chance of separating a mouthful, the way they stretched. Nor were metal chopsticks any help when it came to getting a grip on these slithery things. I offered what I hoped was a reassuring smile to the businessman as he left.

The cook was watching through a hatch, and she came over and sympathetically replaced the metal chopsticks with wooden ones, but I still couldn't pull off a few mouth-sized strands. A surreptitious attempt to use my fingers made an awful mess. People averted their eyes. Never having used large scissors to eat noodles, I just couldn't bring myself to pick them up, knowing I was bound to make a huge, embarrassing faux pas, and – worse – worried they were some kind of misguided concession to my western ineptness with chopsticks. Yet when I managed to shove a noodle into my mouth, I felt like a kid sucking at her first string of spaghetti and wondering breathlessly when it was going to end. It didn't want to break. I had to bite down hard on each thin strand with my front teeth to get it loose.

Finally, after in this inelegant fashion I had got part of this odd-tasting food of cold broth and bungee-noodles into my stomach, a family sat down at a nearby table and ordered the same thing, and I saw them take up the big scissors and cut up the noodles into pieces. The mystery was solved, sort of. But I was fascinated that anyone would invent a noodle so resilient it has to be served with garden shears.

When you travel, exploring restaurants is usually part of the fun. Even when you don't know the language, it's hard to imagine being scared of going to a restaurant. But I'd started to realise that Korea could be very different.

CHAPTER FOUR:

MANY, MANY FAT AMERICANS!

During thirty-five years of Japanese occupation from 1910, Korean culture was crushed; some Koreans went into exile, and many others were tortured and killed. Koreans found this particularly humiliating because they had always considered themselves superior or at least equal to the Japanese, having even introduced them to Buddhism. Yet according to Bruce Cumings in Korea's Place in the Sun, *'almost every westerner supported Japan's "modernising role" in Korea'.*

The Japanese razed Kyungbok Palace in the name of city planning and turned the compound into an administrative centre; the crown prince was sent away to marry a Japanese princess. The Japanese installed their army in Seoul at Yongsan. Able-bodied young

Korean men were taken away to fight Japanese battles across Asia or to labour in mines and war factories. Over 100,000 Korean women were kidnapped and shipped off to Manchuria to serve as 'comfort girls' or 'comfort women', prostitutes for Japanese soldiers. Half of Korea's rice harvest was sent to Japan, leaving people poor and hungry. Koreans were forced to assume Japanese names, language and religion. Richard Storry in A History of Modern Japan *says the Japanese regime in Korea was 'more efficient and in some respects much less arbitrary and harsh than that of the former royal government'; this could also be said of the modern Chinese occupation of Tibet, which is internationally condemned today. Storry says it was 'rigid, severe, unimaginative, and dedicated to an almost hopeless ideal – namely the integration of the Koreans with the Japanese'. The Japanese occupation lasted until 15 August 1945, when at the end of World War Two the dropping of atomic bombs on Nagasaki and Hiroshima forced Japan to surrender to the Allied Forces.*

After only a few years of peace and freedom, however, Korea would be plunged into war, and the Japanese economy would do well out of that, too.

It wasn't an unusual noodle dish that caused the first bout of stomach problems to strike, but a dodgy snack late one night from the famous Egg Sandwich Lady in Hooker Hill, where we roamed after a night of dancing at Hollywood. In the early hours, Gav couldn't resist a fried egg sandwich, and it did him no good.

For the first day, he simply felt unwell. But he made it to work to play the full four sets, dashing to the bathroom in between. By the third day, he lay in bed shivering and pale under several blankets and two army sleeping bags, although it was now early June and swelteringly hot. Every hour or so he would rush to study the bathroom fixtures – which had the brand label Nam Jon, giving rise to the quip that he was doing a tour of Nam – then stagger weakly back to bed. An increasingly frustrated Florence Nightingale in our little flat day after day, I couldn't go out and leave him, and couldn't do much to help except offer sympathy. I wished he'd either call a doctor or say he'd be fine and didn't need me there. Eventually, he went to see a doctor recommended by the hotel, who X-rayed him, diagnosed something vague and gave him a large bill and a variety of medications. The fish oil just made him sick, but we hoped the other stuff would clear up whatever he had.

Summer had begun, and it was sunny, but the city air in Seoul could be oppressively smog-laden, the humidity seeming to trap the traffic fumes. There was another smell: rubbish piled in bags at the roadside waiting for the truck to take them away. It could send out quite a reek as the days got warmer. In the evenings, electric fans whirred.

Luckily, our apartment was on the steep lower slope of Namsan, or South Mountain; a few near-vertical steps from our doorstep was the main road that winds around the mountain, and beyond that an expanse of green park and trees. On the Friday evening, needing exercise and space after days sitting around doing nothing, I took a walk up the hill.

The steep paths were rough but much frequented. Crooked pines had shed a carpet of needles on the ground. Rounding a bend, I came across a clearing and was surprised to see an outdoor gym. If everyone was young and in Spandex, you'd think it was New York perhaps, but no. A woman in her sixties massaged her limbs before going back to lifting a bench-press. Men were doing sit-ups and pull-ups; others were sitting around playing chess. Kids played hula-hoop, and a few old folks waited to fill plastic jugs with water from a spring. How bizarre. I stopped and looked down on the city far below. The grey sky was assuming a tinge of red, and the wide river, the Hangang, gleamed below; the flow and surge of traffic on the bridge now sounded distant. Instead, I was surrounded by magpies and crickets.

I continued and found myself on a road lined with parked cars that wound up the mountain; it passed through pine forest overhung with leafy creepers, and I breathed deeply. There were walkers and joggers, and a family carrying butterfly nets, everyone taking advantage of the peace and quiet. Then I looked into one of the cars, and jumped! People were sleeping inside. Two grey-suited businessmen lay straight back, hands by their sides, sound asleep with their ties firmly in place. There were people sleeping in several of the parked cars, not homeless people but ordinary folk just having a sleep there in public, in their car. How strange.

I carried on up the road to a park at the top. From there I could see to the other side of the city, the smoggy business core with its abundance of office towers. As the sun set, grey department stores started lighting up, transforming into brilliant neon palaces. Among the clutter of buildings, the Chongno Tower stood out: an office high-rise with a big square cut out in the middle. From up here I could also see the craggy mountains that ringed the city.

I wandered by the remnants of Seoul's old fortress walls, originally built around the city in 1395 after Seoul became the capital. They were reinforced in 1422 by King Sejong, the progressive monarch who introduced the phonetic alphabet, and then again a few centuries later. Here was an old beacon signal station that would have used smoke by day or torches by night to signal danger, connected to a countrywide network. There were five stone beacon stands; one would be lit to show 'situation normal', two for 'enemy across border', three for 'enemy approaching', four for 'border violated' and five for 'battle'. But most of the city walls were demolished by the Japanese occupying forces in the early part of the twentieth century in the name of modern city planning, during Korea's liberation in 1945 and during the Korean War.

It wasn't entirely natural or peaceful up on top of Namsan – many people had driven up the hill to visit the museum or theatre or the cafe and to get up close to the Seoul Tower, a modern, utilitarian observation tower that served as a city landmark. Families and couples wandered about decked out in dresses and golf shirts, availing themselves of the activities or the panoramic views. But I liked having this forest-covered mountain, with its thick woods and exercise areas, rising up right in the middle of the city; and clearly, so did everyone else.

Hills have always made me feel happy, because I grew up surrounded by them, looking at rugged green hills from my bedroom window. I always feel more comfortable with hills on the horizon. How I'd happily lived in flat Toronto for years I don't know – though I loved the tree-filled ravines that criss-crossed the city, and my favourite spot for a long time was the old quarry that had been turned into a wetland, with the sides of the Don Valley rising all around. When I'd taught English in Athens after finishing university, I liked to climb up the steep hill in my neighbourhood until I could see right over the jumbled mass of buildings, clouded in pollution, to the surrounding mountains and the harbour of Piraeus beyond, with the ships heading out to sea.

I felt a surge of relief just being up here. Now that the initial excitement was over, Seoul seemed overwhelming – big and congested, the humidity tiring. I was leading a strange existence, between the surreal atmosphere of the Hyatt and a city neighbourhood just going about its business. I'd been before to places that weren't used to tourists. But I'd forgotten what hard work they could be. Had I made the wrong decision by coming to a big, difficult city?

I remembered when I went to Riga, the capital of Latvia, a few years earlier with my then-boyfriend who was translating computer programs. When I arrived, I couldn't believe I was spending my three weeks of holiday in such a grim place. What had I done? Everywhere it was damp and freezing and dark, smelly and dirty and unfriendly. Warned it would be wet, I'd brought an umbrella, not realising they meant several feet of snow would be melting around my feet. The food was revolting – *please, have some more eels in jelly* – and I had no sympathy from my boyfriend, who'd grown up in a Latvian family. There were so many potholes in the street and cars dashing madly around corners, I hardly dared look up; but when I started to, I realised how beautiful the buildings were.

Then one evening, we were invited to a seventieth birthday party. Vera and her husband lived in four tiny unheated rooms of an otherwise empty old collective building: their bed had been folded back into a couch, and a table folded out to seat ten people. The other guests were from a farm, and spoke Latvian, Russian and German, none of which were any good to me, so we communicated by raising a toast every few minutes, knocking back a sherry glass brim-full of vodka. We drank bottle after bottle of the stuff. Soon, I was dancing waltzes with farmers who spoke Russian to me, and looking out over one of the most beautiful views of an old European city I have ever seen. That evening changed everything, and I started to enjoy Latvia.

If I could find the heart of Riga, I could find the soul of Seoul. It was a challenge, but I needn't be so impatient: I was learning, slowly. It was just a question of meeting the people behind the faceless city, and finding its secrets. I breathed in deeply, and walked back down the mountain, ready to try harder.

Gav recovered from his stomach sickness thanks to the medicine, so we spent an afternoon at another of Seoul's old palaces, Changdokkung. There a sprightly pensioner wearing a checked shirt and khaki trousers, a sporty waistcoat with many pockets and a mobile phone on a cord around his neck offered to take our photograph. He introduced himself as 'Mistah Lee' and politely started asking us questions about our visit to Korea. Then he kindly guided us around the gardens, pointing out particular trees and buildings and birds. He mentioned in passing that he'd grown up during the Japanese occupation, and had had to learn Japanese in school, a very different language from Korean. From time to time, Mistah Lee asked, 'Can you understand my English?'

'Oh yes,' we said. It was perfect, and we were delighted to have met this interesting man. 'It's excellent!'

'Ah, thank you, thank you, you are very kind.' He explained that he used to work for a bank, and had been sent to work in Washington for a while, which was where he'd learned English. It had also been an eye-opening experience.

'Many, many fat Americans!' he exclaimed, with a shocked expression. 'They walk like this' – he waddled, pigeon-toed, hands out front as if holding a big stomach. 'I think it is a big problem in America?'

'Well, ahem, yes,' we replied. 'There are quite a lot of large people in America... There's a definite problem there, apparently.' We were about to move on when Mr Lee spotted a Korean child of about ten, somewhat on the plump side, kneeling over the edge of a fishpond.

'Oooh, fat boy!' he said, pointing openly. 'Very fat!' We nodded sheepishly, hoping the poor boy wasn't taking English at school. It was quite unusual to see fat people in

Seoul. Some of the young women were extremely thin, but even older women tended to stay trim, as did the men.

Mr Lee explained that he had stayed in shape since his retirement by climbing mountains, like many Koreans, and he was proud of it. Over six per cent of the country was national park, mostly mountains and coastal areas. He suggested we visit Pukansan, a national park that could be reached via underground train from Seoul. We'd read about it but weren't sure exactly how to get there, and the underground train system was so complex – but now I knew it was time to make the effort. He drew a little map in my notebook, which showed we should take Line 3 of the subway to Kupabal Station, and a bus from there. Before saying goodbye, he also gave us his HP, his 'hand-phone' number, in case we needed any help during our stay in Korea.

The highest point of Pukansan National Park was at 837 metres, over three times the height of Namsan, and some of the park's trails could take days to complete and involve serious climbing, while others closer to the city could be done easily in a few hours. At Namdaemun Market we acquired a tent and a water bottle – army surplus and very cheap with a bit of haggling. We had to keep reminding ourselves they wouldn't sell unless they were making something on it. At Yongsan Electronics Market, we'd asked the price of a set of stereo speakers and were told 50,000 won, so we thanked the vendor and walked away, at which point he instantly said, 'OK, twenty thousand.'

Getting up early on a Sunday was becoming difficult with Gav's nocturnal schedule, which I was naturally adopting. The novelty of staying up late every night and losing the morning was wearing thin, especially as I didn't have a band to play in. Around lunchtime on this particular Sunday we strolled down the road to the Hyatt to find a taxi. As Itaewon Station was still being built, our nearest subway station was Samgakchi, beyond the US army base. We got in the back of the cab, said '*Annyung haseyo*', and, smiling sweetly, I announced: 'Samgakchi, *chuseyo!*'

The driver looked blank, clearly not understanding.

'Samgakchi,' I repeated, enunciating slowly and carefully. '*Chuseyo*,' I added, 'please.'

Still nothing.

'Samgakchi, samgakchi.' That *was* the name of the closest underground station, right?

No movement. In fact, he was getting a bit pissed off.

'Sam-gak-chi,' I tried, very slowly. Gav said no, it's better to say it quickly, and in forceful rapid fire repeated: 'Samgakchi.'

'Ah, Samgakchi!' With this, he gave a withering look, which seemed to say, if you'd just told me you wanted to go to Samgakchi in the first place, I'd have taken you there right away. I sat back, determined not to be defeated. The language was proving a little more difficult than it had first appeared. Although I could slowly spell out words on a page, proper pronunciation was eluding me, and sentence construction was a long way off. I was determined to get by in Korean. I'd studied Ancient Greek and Old English, for heaven's sake.

We passed the imposing War Museum. A wide sweep of steps led towards the long building, which had a dome over the grand but futuristic entranceway, and the Korean flag flying proudly. At the front of the building, stands were being built for the coming commemoration ceremonies. The hopeful euphoria that was, according to the English-language *Korea Herald*, overtaking the Koreas with the coming of the 14 July peace summit, had clearly not reached Seoul's taxi drivers.

A standard undergound train fare of 950 won would take you anywhere in the city, including Kupabal. From there, we took a short bus ride to the village on the edge of Pukansan. The sun was shining through the haze. While I'd enjoyed the space that Namsan afforded, it felt so blissfully good to get right away from the city, from the draining experience the simplest conversation or transaction could turn into, as this morning had shown. Here it was just mountains and sunshine. Just inside the park were cool, sparkling rock pools. Families were picnicking on the smooth, flat rocks, and kids were jumping in the water below restaurants with shady terraces. Idyllic as it was, we pressed on until the day-tripping crowds thinned out, and took a path uphill. The city traffic still provided a faint hum in the background. A carpet of thick green trees rose gradually into jutting, rocky peaks. The trail struck steeply up the hillside. Hikers wearing multi-pocketed sporty waistcoats and colourful socks passed us on their way up or down and shouted cheery hellos, *annyung haseyo!*

Suddenly, I turned a corner and saw a Buddhist statue the height of eight men standing in the midst of a tiny temple. The serene white figure looked out from the hillside over the gleaming, lush, green valley. The quiet was palpable. The tiny temple Dugamsa was little more than a lawn scattered with carved stones, a man-sized bronze bell in its own little pavilion, and the statue. We lingered awhile.

From there, steep stone steps followed the wall of the ancient fortress, Pukansansong, first built in AD132, all the way up the side of the mountain to the peak of Wonhyobong. It was hot and tiring, and unfortunately we'd only brought one large bottle of water, which was depleting and fast warming up as we took gasping breaks in the hot afternoon. 'Brought any teabags?' quipped Gav. The other, army-issue water bottle we'd filled usefully with duty-free Irish whisky.

The backpack dragged at my shoulders. But despite the agonies of the climb, when we reached the summit, the vistas were joyfully dramatic: glistening pine-green valleys spreading out between bare white rounded granite peaks. The mountains were not high, but their steep sides made them impressive. We sprawled out on the smooth slabs of rock, sweating and exhausted – but thrilled.

As dusk began to fall, we knew we wouldn't make it to the nearest designated shelter, so we discreetly set up our little tent between some trees a short distance off the path. It was less a two-man tent than a tent for two people who know each other very well. We had tinned tuna and bread and some sips of whisky, saving the rest of the water for the morning. Giggling, and not finding the sleeping mats very effective at masking the bumps in the ground, we fell asleep to the strange and soothing sound of drums and bells rising up the side of the mountain from the temple below. As the sun rose in the morning, a man began singing at the top of his voice from the nearby peak. This was what I had come here for – and I wanted more.

CHAPTER FIVE:

HOW I LEARNED TO LOVE KIMCHI

Back in Seoul, life was a far cry from the beauty of Pukansan.

Some evenings I'd go along to see part of the show at the Hyatt, and between sets Gav and I sat by the changing rooms to chat. I tended not to stay long, though. The music didn't change much, and it's awkward standing in a bar on your own when you can't afford to buy a drink.

Good Vibes weren't getting along all that well. Shauna and Vinny had a bad start when they had an affair early on that turned sour, and Shauna threw a cup of hot chocolate at Vinny in the hushed and proper Hyatt dining room, behaving as if she were Whitney Houston, not just the hotel band's requisite female. Perhaps she was very upset, but there was something about being adored by an audience, especially when they were rich businessmen and high-ranking army officers, that went to people's heads and made them act differently. I thought it amusing, but Gav was angry because he felt, as a member of the same group, he'd be seen in the same light. Occasionally, we'd offer a spare couch to someone from another band on the hotel circuit who'd been ripped off for their final pay cheque or fired for no reason. The only person who never complained about anything was Leroy, who just grinned and said 'Yeah yeah yeah!' and practised his dance moves.

Dean had been leading Good Vibes for years and was determined at last to make a success of it. For a larger cut of the takings, he made all the business decisions and dealt with the booking agents. After this three-month gig, there would be others; it was just a question of what the agents could find them. Except for Gav and Shauna, in their early twenties, the others were a bit too old to make it as real stars, but I was learning that there is a subculture of D-list musicians who make a perfectly decent living around the world without anyone having heard of them. All these guys were eager to give up their back-home jobs as used-car salesmen and small-time landlords, and play music full-time. Who wouldn't?

Gav showed up to every rehearsal, hoping they could expand their repertoire, maybe a U2 number, nothing outlandish. Mostly, though, nobody else showed up, and they blamed him for not knowing they'd rescheduled because he hadn't been spending enough time with them.

They figured I was keeping him from having a good time with his mates in the band, making me feel guilty for being there, although Gav had no doubts he'd rather spend his days with his new girlfriend than his workmates. But Gav could get along with most people, and we often went out with them for drinks at Hollywood or King Club late at night, where everyone would drink shots of tequila until Dean started complaining and calling everyone 'muthafuckas'.

The latest rift was because Dean wanted to invest a third of next month's salaries on some new stage costumes. Gav couldn't understand why, when he was stuck at the back of the stage almost hidden behind his drum kit, he still had to wear cringe-making Eurovision-style shiny trousers and two-tone shimmery sleeveless T-shirts. Poor dear. The only person who actually looked good in these costumes was Shauna, who had spectacular breasts thanks to the enhancement operation she'd had just before coming out here, and had her costumes cut extra tight, so skimpy that even I would watch mesmerised just to see if the thin strips of material would stay in place as she danced up on stage.

Gav had been playing in bands since school, winning Battle of the Bands competitions and taking master classes. He hit the drums hard, and sometimes sticks broke during a set, but he was a master of switching to a new one without losing a beat. Now and again he'd need to re-stock on sticks from the music centre at Nagwon. It was a huge multi-level arcade full of music shops – guitars, drums, amps, pianos, every kind of instrument. People were always re-stringing guitars or trying out sounds, cleaning pianos and tubas. I have never been musical, although I love dancing, so Gav's proverbial candy shop where he tested drumsticks and ogled guitars and DM5 amps bored me silly. But then we emerged and made our way through the maze of faceless buildings and the sea of people to explore the city.

We decided to visit another kind of musical landmark, the place where ancient Korean music was played once a year, Intangible Cultural Property Number One. The Chongmyo Shrine, like Kyungbokkung, was another island of calm and symbol of national pride, set back from city hustle and bustle by expanses of pale stone courtyard. Stretching across one end was a low hall painted deep red, with a tall, sombre roof made of dark grey pottery tiles. Behind the locked red doors of the hall were the spirit tablets of all the kings and queens of the Choson Dynasty.

The Choson Dynasty lasted from 1392, when Seoul became capital, for five hundred years. The name Choson, meaning 'land of the morning calm', was given by the Chinese, who saw the sun rise from Korea's misty mountains. The ruling elite of the Choson Dynasty respected China as the home of their political ideology and the guiding principles of life, Confucianism. Advocating education, obedience, discipline and ancestor worship, Confucianism remains one of the guiding principles of Korean life.

The Choson Dynasty's golden age, seen as the high point of Korean civilisation, was the reign of King Sejong the Great, whose phonetic alphabet replaced the complex 3,000 picture symbols of Chinese. Today literacy in South Korea rests at nearly ninety-nine per cent, helped by the Confucian respect for education. Other Korean inventions during the fifteenth century included moveable metal type, which produced books on farming and medicine to spread learning; Korean printers mastered this technique several years before Gutenberg, and thousands of books were produced. It was a time when the sciences and the arts thrived, a pinnacle of scientific and technological achievement.

Back out on the streets, we found ourselves at Chongno Samga, the busy intersection in the commercial centre of the city, and ready to eat. After the incident with the noodles and the scissors, I'd been loath to risk restaurants, but it was time to try again. I'd learned of a dish called *bibimbap*, vegetables with rice, popular with westerners. We found a place that looked simple and innocuous and walked in.

The woman in charge, wiry with short curly hair, immediately told us to leave. 'Only Korean food,' she explained.

'It's OK,' said Gav, and I smiled. 'We want Korean food!'

Eyeing us suspiciously, she let us sit down at a table. In due course, a young waitress walked towards us to take our order, but suddenly she blushed, put her hand over her mouth, started giggling uncontrollably and ran back into the kitchen.

It was perplexing, in the centre of a capital city of a first-world industrialised nation. We waited, and the older lady came back and agreed to bring us *bibimbap* – warning that it would be 'ferry, ferry hhat!'

It arrived and looked delicious: a bowl of white rice, around which colourful vegetables were arranged in sections – grated carrot, slivers of cucumber, wilted spinach and long thin enoki mushrooms – with a blob of hot red sauce and a fried egg in the middle. I grabbed my chopsticks and started to tuck in when the bossy woman returned. She whisked the chopsticks out of my hand and thrust a metal spoon in my right hand instead.

Was my performance with chopsticks so awful? Our host gestured towards all the other diners who were using their spoons for *bibimbap*. Then she showed us that you take the spoon and mash all the ingredients together until the whole lot is covered in red sauce, and eat it with a spoon only. You had to laugh. We mashed up our *bibimbap* like good little children, and ate it all up. It was full of intense flavours and distinct textures – wonderful.

I was beginning to realise Korean culture had many rules of etiquette; discipline and obedience were revered; breaking the rules just wasn't done. Rice dishes in Korea are eaten with a spoon, and that's that. Chopsticks are for side dishes and noodles.

Our road didn't have a name, or at least there weren't any street signs, and we couldn't figure out how to explain exactly where we lived. To get home, we'd ask the taxi driver for the *Hyattu Hotelo*, because everyone knew where that was; so he'd take the road that wound up around Namsan towards the Hyatt, and then when we got close to where we lived we'd shout *yogio!* And the poor confused driver would ask *yogio?* And we'd assure him yes, here, thrust 1,000-won notes in his hand, and jump out before the traffic behind starting beeping their horns.

The cost of living in Seoul was similar to back home, and nights out could cost a lot more, which made me anxious every time I withdrew my savings. Withdrawing money wasn't all that easy, though. I'd brought only plastic, assuming that everywhere in the world was hooked up to the same system these days, and that traveller's cheques were an outmoded thing only benighted old yokels carried around. Surely in technologically advanced Korea, the home of the electronic gadget, taking out cash with my bank card wouldn't be a problem. The bank machines showed all the right symbols for my bank card, but they'd spit out the alien bit of plastic, suggesting I try another machine elsewhere.

One Sunday evening, we took a taxi to a new area of the city, ready to explore. We spotted a bank machine but it returned our cards in disgust. There was a more promising row of machines across the road, but the road had six lanes of speeding traffic and you weren't supposed to cross it without using a special walkway. We found the walkway, trekked all the way over, and had the same humiliating response from each of the bank machines.

'It'll be fine,' said Gav.

'How do you know it will be fine?' I replied.

We spent most of the evening walking from bank machine to bank machine. We thought maybe we'd go and see a film, but couldn't figure out how to get in to the cinema. Eventually we ate terrible pizza, the only meal we could afford, and went back to Itaewon defeated.

The machines in the Hyatt *did* accept international cards – but only until a certain time of day. If they were out of service, there was another at the Hilton, and one in

Myungdong – but you could count on one hand the number of bank machines in this enormous city that accepted foreign bank cards, and they tended to be out of service half the time. They didn't tell you *that* in the *Welcome to Korea* magazine. It didn't make you feel very welcome.

Not wanting to spend extravagantly anyway, in the evenings I'd kiss Gav goodbye as he strode out the door listening to music to gear himself up for the show, then I'd go out for a long walk – just pick a direction and go hunting for adventure. When I lived in Athens, an evening stroll around town would generally yield a few smiles, bizarre conversations, the occasional invitation to join in someone's party, some little epiphany about Greek life. Whenever I felt lonely and down there, I'd just go for a walk and see what cropped up. I'd found the same in Georgetown, Guyana. I was told it was far too dangerous for me to go out on my own, as a white woman; that if I were to venture into the Stabroek Market on my own I'd be either mugged or killed. For a week or two I stayed obediently in the compound. And then I got bored, and started walking – and, of course, found friendly people as I watched the real life of the city happening around me.

Here in Seoul, from the road that wound around Namsan I'd look out across the lights of the sprawling city, punctuated by the huge TV screens of electronic billboards. I'd find my way into different neighbourhoods, watching how people went about their lives, like the old man I saw who was beating the heat of the summer night by moving his bed outside and sleeping on the road. But making contact wasn't easy in Seoul. I could wander around for hours and smile at strangers, but most people seemed not to notice me. In a world where nobody says hello, life can be pretty dull. Be open-minded, I told myself, lose your expectations, be patient, keep trying.

Later, I'd go down the hill to a local 'PC bang' (computer room) called Click where I emailed friends and family back home, and wrote down my thoughts and impressions. It was cheap at 2,000 won per hour, and open all night; this was before Internet cafes cropped up everywhere in the world, and this innovative phenomenon was proving hugely popular in Korea, having grown from one hundred rooms to 15,000 in the last two years. They were situated in every neighbourhood of the city and were filled with Korean youth, who went there to play computer games on the high-speed lines and chat on their hand-phones and chain-smoke. I sat amid clouds of cigarette smoke and the electronic simulations of gunfight as young people in headphones shot each other's characters to pieces, the noises interrupted every few minutes by the jangle of a phone and the subsequent '*Yoboseyo? Yoboseyo?*'

Sunday was the only evening I had with Gav, and we crammed a whole week's worth into it. The next Sunday, we stocked up on cash first and visited a district that supposedly had theatre and street entertainment. But however much we searched for something cultural, we only found bars and restaurants. By the evening, however, we had made the important linguistic discovery that *hopu* or *hof* indicated draft beer, which was cheaper than bottled beer, and therefore fun to drink. Sitting in a bar was always good fun anyway, because Gav had the proverbial Irish gift of the gab and the two of us could spend hours just talking away.

It was the morning after this night on the *hof* that I learned to love kimchi.

Of course I'd tried it from the beginning: it's an essential requirement of Korean cuisine, the national dish, a staple of the diet. Korean couples sometimes take a kimchi-making course before they get married, and there are summer kimchi-making contests. But at first, kimchi strikes you as a distinctly acquired taste. It's made of Chinese cabbage soaked in brine and rinsed, then layered with a mix of green onions, garlic, soy sauce or shellfish sauce, ginger, salt and lots of hot red pepper powder or flakes, which is all left to ferment as a pungent red mess. A family's supply of kimchi was traditionally kept in a big glazed jar and buried in the ground through the cold winter as a stash of goodness. It has vitamin A and calcium, more vitamin C than a fresh apple, it breaks down fats in the body, is low in calories and high in fibre, and has all sorts of immunising properties helpful against cancer and heart disease. It comes as a complimentary side dish with every meal, so you keep trying it. And you think, 'Hmm, still not sure'.

Then one day you discover its usefulness as a hangover cure. You just know it's the best thing you can put into your body. It's salty, spicy and full of crunchy vegetable goodness, like a bloody mary you eat with chopsticks, and it gets to work right away on curing that fuzzy headache and queasy stomach. Before you know it, you can't get enough: you're hooked on kimchi. You're ordering extra. You know it makes sense. Comfort me with kimchi.

There are many different kinds, depending on the vegetables used and the length of the aging; instead of cabbage you can use crunchy radishes, tiny ones or chunks called *kaktugi*, and you can have fresh or sour kimchi, plain or watery. You can have *kimchi ramyun*, the spicy instant noodles we'd taken a liking to, or *kimchi tchigae*, the stew with tofu and meat. To most Koreans, a meal without kimchi is unthinkable. It's kimchi, and not variety, that's the spice of Korean life. And now I was hooked. It had to be a good sign that I would find the heart of Seoul sometime soon.

CHAPTER SIX:

DARK NIGHT OF MY SEOUL

It was 11 p.m. in this city of eleven million people, and I was still just trying to meet one or two of them. I was on my own in something that called itself a 'Beer Restaurant' between one of the universities and the fashion district of Myungdong, drinking a beer and eating popcorn. It was a busy place full of voices and laughter, suits and office shirts, an after-work sort of place. The floor was strewn with food and cigarette butts and paper napkins. It reminded me a bit of a tapas bar in Spain. And yet not quite, because – ah yes, there you go – people don't spit on the floor quite as much in Spain. Here it was quite the national pastime. The received wisdom was that it got rid of the bad humours in the body, or something; surely the reality was that it spread them around?

Cold beer and big plates of food were dispensed from a bar in the corner. The beer, '"Live" by Hite: Three Filtering Non-pasteurization', was described on the glass as so fresh and clean, made with pure spring water ('Health! Fresh!'), you'd think it was good for you. But at the table behind me, two men were asleep, heads down on the table. At the table in front, two red-faced men in golf shirts argued loudly with smokers' voices. Ten young guys came in, short black spiky hair and phones hung around their necks. They shuffled chairs and pushed tables together, ordered food and drinks from the waiter; then one of them fell asleep, and they all stumbled out again ten minutes later, leaving beers and fruit plate barely touched. As the volume rose, one of the sleeping men behind me woke up and staggered heavily out the door, trying to drag his friend with him quite literally. One of the ten young men returned to search clumsily under the table for something, probably a phone, no doubt now mired in the phlegm and napkins and cigarette ends.

I looked on amused but slightly bemused: was this the only city in the world where a lone, ostensibly eligible female could walk into a bar and have no one to talk to? OK, so I was wearing a ring on my wedding finger, but that's not usually a major deterrent to banter and flirtatious chit-chat. It wasn't that they hadn't noticed the only person in the room whose hair wasn't black. I was so evidently not from around these parts, and I was trying to smile and look approachable. You don't realise how nice a little attention is, how much it contributes to your sense of self, until it's not there. I could hardly blame the good men of Seoul for that: I was taller than most of them, and felt grotesquely fat compared to the women, many of whom were wafer-slim, graceful, immaculate and beautiful with their long, straight black hair. There were a few women in this room, hanging out with their office mates, most of them oddly frumpy but animated. I was too big in general for this town, and too scruffy. My long brown hair was getting unbecomingly wavy up in the humidity so one day I took the scissors to it in the bathroom, thinking short might be cool. No, it still frizzed. Not very hana-sum. My skin was pasty white from the smoggy city air. I felt awkward, unnatural, unsexed.

I'd been in Seoul for almost a month, but I wasn't meeting any people. It was partly because of the language barrier, though if no one spoke English, you had to wonder why the beer labels were in English. Some people stared, others completely ignored me, but hardly anyone smiled or said hello. It was nigh on impossible to learn anything first-hand about people's lives.

Seoul was impersonal, like all big cities, three times the size of any other city I'd lived in: people going to and from their offices, intent on business, and although in the evenings they evidently loosened up a bit, it didn't make them any more friendly to outsiders. To be barely curious about foreigners – when there were so few here – struck me as odd. Was it against the rules of Korean etiquette? Maybe it was national pride, this lack of interest in the West, which you have to commend, of course – who needs the West? Perhaps especially in a country that had had a US army presence for fifty years.

I took a book out of my bag and started reading, making notes. Could South Korea still have traces of its Hermit

Kingdom past, its policy of isolation, mistrusting and excluding foreigners? For centuries after the devastating Japanese invasions of 1592–1598, Korea was allied with China but refused entry to other foreigners, became like a hermit. Even in the 1800s, when Roman Catholic priests came with trade ships from Europe to this part of the world, their learning was seen as a threat. The British East India Company sent a ship to Korea, and it was turned away on the grounds that it contravened Korean laws to engage in foreign commerce. There was a 'closed door' policy. That's all long in the past. Yet the twentieth century wasn't kind to Korea.

A successful peace summit talk had just occurred between the leaders of North and South Korea in Pyongyang, the capital of North Korea. The resulting 15 June Joint Declaration committed them to arranging reunions of a number of divided families later in the summer. A lottery would determine one hundred families who could meet briefly with their loved ones from the other side of the border. The leaders agreed to work closely for inter-Korean cooperation.

No wonder there was the sense in South Korea of a new era beginning. People hadn't come here for pleasure for a long time. But the next year, 2001, was official Visit Korea Year. President Kim Dae-jung's message to the people, as quoted in the first issue of *Welcome to Korea*, was very optimistic: 'The development of the tourism industry will attract foreign currency and help promote a positive image of the country, ultimately laying the foundation for world peace.'

World peace, eh? Well, let's give it a try. I strolled outside. There were already young men sitting on the kerb with their heads on their knees, surrendered to a combination of weariness and alcohol. Myungdong, a busy shopping district by day, now looked deserted. You couldn't just wander the streets looking for a lively scene. Bars and restaurants lurked in basements or third-floors of square commercial buildings behind dark, tinted windows. And behind pulsating neon signs that seemed to promise wild abandon, I found only sedate lounges with cosy sofas and coffee tables, where a few people were talking quietly. I looked around for people who might be approachable, but they were all wrapped up in their own worlds. I didn't know how to find the soul of Seoul. The busiest places I'd seen on a Friday night were the PC bang.

Oh god, what was I doing here? I was learning, but it was awfully hard. I walked back in the direction of home. I supposed I'd meet people if I was working, and wouldn't be as worried about money, yet after seven years of slogging away at a career, I wasn't interested in getting a job teaching English, although it would probably be possible. But everyone around me was working, and I was losing my self-confidence. It had been a strange role reversal: Gav had gone from being a university dropout and unappreciated bartender to working his dream job as a professional musician entertaining grateful audiences every night, while I'd gone from being incessantly in demand to completely invisible.

Now that summer had arrived, the air was muggy and the streets smelled. The rain hadn't been enough to wash the streets clean, only to wet the rubbish and start some sort of rotting process. I remembered now being told that it got damp enough for mildew to grow on your clothes. Walking home, I reached the Hyatt around 2 a.m. and so decided to wait for Gav to come out after the show, so we could walk home together. As I stood on the roadside opposite the entrance, a car stopped and a man tried to make conversation through the open window, asking how old I was. When I ignored him and he left, another man in a blue van drew up and – I realised I'd better not stand here again in what to normal people is the middle of the night. Not the kind of attention I'd been after. I was getting tired of the stickiness and the sleaze. I needed to get out of town.

When Korea was freed from Japanese rule at the end of World War Two, an agreement made by Britain, the United States and the USSR determined that the northern half of Korea would be temporarily occupied by the USSR and the southern by the US. Korea had little say in the matter: it was a pawn in a game between superpowers. A United Nations commission was set up to install a united government, but talks reached an impasse, and the commission was refused entry to the North. The administration in the South elected a government and then declared independence.

Both sets of foreign troops were withdrawn from North and South. But then the USSR supplied the government in the North with enough weaponry to fit out a powerful army, and it invaded the South in 1950. The Koreans of the North presumably were fighting to reunite their country under their own, now communist, administration. UN troops, mostly American, were brought back to defend the South, but they had little effect. That was until the US general Douglas MacArthur led UN forces in a daring landing at Inchon, which forced the army from the North within a month to withdraw right back to the border of Manchuria. Then China agreed to send masses of troops to support the North, extending the war, and finally driving the Allied Forces back to the thirty-eighth parallel, where the DMZ is now.

The three years of war devastated Korea, ending in a ceasefire and Korea still divided. During the chaos, there was massive movement of people between the North and the South. Some from the South voluntarily joined the North because they believed it was the way to reunify the country. But a line was drawn across the centre of the country, closing off the other half indefinitely. People are still living with the effects. You could easily have a sibling or a child or even a husband or wife on the other side of the border, on the enemy side. Millions in South Korea have relatives in the North.

CHAPTER SEVEN:

SEOUL BY THE SEA

We got into a cab to go to Samgakchi Station, and five minutes later I realised I'd forgotten something essential, so we somehow had to explain to the driver that we needed him to turn back. Of course he couldn't understand why we wanted to go back to the apartment, and to make matters worse, Itaewonno was gridlocked and in chaos. He huffed and tutted as we awkwardly directed him back up a shortcut to the Hyatt. Taxi drivers could be so unpleasant. If they weren't refusing to take you somewhere, they were trying to run you over.

A Sunday by the sea beckoned, however. Inchon, famous as the site of a decisive point in the war, was Seoul's seaport on the Yellow Sea facing China, and reachable by train through the urban sprawl linking the two cities. After the hour-long train ride to Inchon, we took a cab straight to the Wolmido waterfront, one of the landing areas of Douglas MacArthur's UN forces during the Korean War, now said to be a trendy cultural district of street theatre and art galleries, with restaurants and bars overlooking the sea. But how our hopes were dashed. There was a small amusement park or fun fair, and a boardwalk lined with tacky pubs. Worst of all, the sea was dimly grey, flat and uninviting, reflecting a grey sky. Seoul-by-the-sea was trapped in foggy, grey humidity.

It was already early evening. There was no lovely waterfront to walk along, or much to see. We'd desperately wanted to do something different, to enjoy being by the sea, but there seemed nothing but this row of theme bars. What to do? 'Let's just go for a beer,' said Gav. It had been a somewhat tiring journey, especially for Gav, who was constantly exhausted these days. Trying to have a laugh about it, we settled on a pub called 'Bull's Beer', whose theme wavered between cowboy and maritime, with a 'Highway to Heaven' sign on the door that led upstairs to the bar. At a damp table we ordered a jug. Popcorn came in a bucket that looked daubed in engine oil outside and in. But there were views over the sea and islands, and a sunset that you could almost say was turning to gold. For want of something better to do, we ordered another jug of beer. This, it turned out, was our worst idea yet.

I misguidedly veered onto talking about some liaison I'd had in the past. Perhaps I was trying to make myself sound more interesting than I currently felt. It went over badly.

'I know you've had other relationships,' Gav said. 'I'd just rather not hear about them.'

'I wouldn't mind hearing about your previous relationships,' I protested.

'Yes you would,' argued Gav, probably correctly.

'So I'm not allowed to talk about before I met you? I'm not sure I'm happy about that,' I said angrily. Gav, in a patronising tone, told me to control my temper. By and by it developed into a full-scale argument, with me angrily calling him 'Gavin' instead of Gav, and him talking in an annoyingly calm, superior voice, which made me remind him how he was still a youngster, which didn't go down well. We'd been thrown into a strange intimacy – living together in a place where we were reliant on each other, with no friends to let off steam with, when we still barely understood one another.

Abandoning Bull's Beer, we looked around and found a *yogwan*, the Korean equivalent of a pension or motel that, while entirely without charm, was a place to stay and wasn't expensive at 30,000 won. The old woman in charge brought us toothbrushes and a plastic razor, and then began hovering around saying things we didn't understand. We smiled and nodded, but I was desperate to put my backpack down and inadvertently stepped into the room without first removing my shoes and putting on the customary slippers. Her tirade increased in volume and speed, without a pause to see if I had half a clue what she was talking about. Surely it was fairly obvious I didn't understand a word? Why couldn't she just go away and leave us in peace? Hoping she couldn't understand a word I said either, I smiled at her as sweetly as

I could and said, 'Yes, yes, I don't know what you're saying so just fuck off, OK?' Thankfully uncomprehending, she nodded and finally left us. Gav was shocked but amused.

There was a big mirror on the wall right next to the bed, a plastic brown headboard, faux satin bedclothes, rock hard pillows and a lurid purple bathroom. As well as toothbrushes and razor, the management provided hairspray, moisturiser, shampoo and vile-smelling aftershave, all in half-used family-sized containers. There was no sheet on the bed and the towel was barely big enough to dry your face. Once again, you had to laugh. I wistfully thought of the basic but lovely rooms I'd found in seaside towns all over Europe, forgetting that I was supposed to have left my expectations at home. Still, the room provided a weird sort of neutral space, a kind of haven from the craziness out there, and Gav and I made friends again.

When we went out in search of dinner, we found a fairly comfortable restaurant where we ordered *bulgogi*, marinated beef with rice, glasses of *hof*, and some horrible sandwiches on white bread with unidentifiable contents, just because we craved sandwiches. Late at night, drunk, we went back to the *yogwan*, acting silly all the way home and forgetting to buy water.

We woke early the next morning, aghast at how much money we'd spent, wilting in the heat of the room and completely drained of energy. The shower barely worked, obliterating the possibility of feeling fresh and revitalised. When we got outside, the streets were smelly and dirty and the sea looked brown.

Our plan had been to take a ferry to a nearby island, but the islands were totally obscured by a thick fog, which seemed to hang at ground level and stick to your skin. It didn't seem worth the trip. So we continued down the quay, hoping to walk off our hangovers and glum spirits. At the end was the area of, according to an English sign, 'Sliced Law Fish Restaurants'. The letter in *hangul* that denotes 'r' also denotes 'l'. Sushi! The sushi district turned out to be a long alley flanked by two rows of shacks with fish tanks outside, housing octopus, crabs, creeping sea slugs, unidentifiable molluscs and creatures resembling human hearts and orchids. Not the best sight for a queasy stomach. Interesting? Yes. Breakfast? I think not.

Away from the seafront we found ourselves on a road where a coach was parked, and a busload of old folks had laid mats across the pavement. Women were squatting on the mats preparing bowls of kimchi, beans and fish. I smiled to see them enjoying themselves, and they beckoned me over and asked if we wanted to eat. I couldn't have eaten a thing, but it was a heartwarming, redeeming moment.

Life in South Korea hasn't been easy for a long time. As the nation was recovering from the post-war years, it fell under the sway of a succession of anti-communist military regimes that suppressed personal freedom. Attempts were made on the lives of those who protested against the system, including the young Kim Dae-jung.

After the assassination of the military president General Park Chung-hee in 1979 – by the director of the Korean Central

Intelligence Agency, who claimed he was impeding the path to democracy — came censorship and martial law, and a brutal incident that can only be likened to the Tiananmen Square massacre. In Kwangju in May 1980, a rebellion against the infringement of freedom by police and militia led first to beatings, then to mutilations and killings. The deaths of ordinary people were officially said to be 200, but were later proven to be closer to 2,000. And the American commander-in-chief was implicated for condoning the withdrawal of troops from the border to deal with the rebellion.

Kim Dae-jung was accused of being a communist and instigating the uprising, and was sentenced to death by court martial. He was abducted, held prisoner in a basement cell, unable to see daylight for sixty days, living with his interrogators in the same cell. He was naked and could hear the cries of pain from torture taking place in adjoining cells. 'Under those circumstances, one can turn anybody into a communist,' he has written. South Korea's international reputation was severely tainted.

The eighties for many South Koreans were a period of struggling and fighting for justice. There were secret police tapping phones and beating up anyone they perceived to be a radical. People were not allowed to travel abroad except for business or study. When Seoul hosted the 1988 Olympics, Kim Dae-jung encouraged the world to boycott them. He was accused of trying to overthrow the state, and spent three years in prison and three under house arrest, then went abroad, conducting research at Cambridge, where he wrote The Launching of Many Beginnings. His inauguration as president, in 1998, marked the first peaceful transfer of power.

Considering South Koreans couldn't freely leave the country until 1989, no wonder they found foreigners unapproachably weird.

On the train back to Seoul, the carriage filled up quickly with an oddball cast. A giggly young woman sat beside me and slapped my face with her ponytail every time she turned to her friend. Another woman stared into her pocket mirror unblinkingly for ten minutes straight. Next to her, a skinnny old man asleep with his mouth open slowly fell sideways until he was leaning on her shoulder. Further down the carriage was a suave young fashion victim wearing black drainpipe trousers, a diamanté fake Chanel watch, and crocodile 'long shoes', as I called them. 'Long shoes' were a wildly popular current trend, whereby your shoes are trodden down at the heel and clownishly long in the toes. They seemed to go along with 'long trousers', trousers that were way too long, in a cumbersome way. Perhaps it was something to do with trying to look taller, in the way Tokyo girls were supposed to favour really big platform shoes.

I was relieved to be back in Seoul. The onslaught of multiple lanes of mad traffic, the cab driver who refused to take us from the station to the Hyatt – somehow they seemed pleasingly familiar, sophisticated and cosmopolitan.

That evening, after Gav went to work, I found an elegant cafe in Itaewon, further down where the street became less seedy and more expensive. I decided to treat myself. I sipped a cafe latte and a chilled blue glass of water at a spotless glass table, which held a little dish containing two perfect floating pink flowers, each a subtle shade different. People spoke in hushed tones and there was soothing classical violin playing on the stereo. The place was called The Espresso Coffee Club, and its slogan was 'Best Taste – Since 2000'. A venerable institution. Well, they got my vote. They even gave me a free peanut cookie. I relaxed, happy to be on my own.

I'd mostly travelled alone before. Travelling with someone, you never really leave your own culture behind. You never forget who you are. You are more concerned about having a good time than stretching yourself. I needed that stretching experience. Gav didn't have the same sense that there was something missing. Drumming is physically demanding, and Gav was waking up exhausted, his back aching, needing rest. And in the best of circumstances, Gav was happy just reading the paper all day, while I needed to be out and about and active. Maybe it was partly our age difference: I perhaps felt more keenly the march of time, and certainly knew how many months it had taken me to earn the cash fund I was steadily depleting here. When I felt like I was wasting my time, it made me bad-tempered.

After touching some nerves in our argument in Inchon, Gav and I had talked calmly about each of us spending a little more time alone. I wanted to see the country. I was excitedly poring over maps, trying to drag Gav out of town on the afternoons and Sundays, when he was torn between wanting the same and needing to relax. Gav had been drumming since his skinny legs would hardly reach the pedals of the bass. He was having fun, and I should too.

I'd worried what time apart might do to our relationship. The first time I left behind a boyfriend to travel, I only lasted a few weeks before meeting someone else. But maybe our time was up then anyway? I was so young then – maybe I'd changed? And our relationship wasn't going to survive anyway at this rate unless something was done. I'd just take a few days at a time, and then come back to Seoul to spend most weekends with Gav.

I needed to find out more about Korea's tantalising ancient traditions, which I'd glimpsed in Seoul at Namdaemun, Chongmyo Shrine, Kyungbok Palace. There must be a happier history than that of the twentieth century. Koreans led mostly a rural existence until only a few decades ago: the countryside was where I needed to start looking for the soul of Korea.

Now that I was planning this, suddenly even Itaewon felt pleasant. It had been raining for hours, clearing the air and cleaning the streets. Perhaps the rain made everyone happier. Even one of the stern guards at an embassy gate on the road up to the Hyatt smiled back at me and said *annyung haseyo*.

PART TWO: MAKING FRIENDS

'*Myself, being in a manner a haphazard loiterer about the world, and prone to linger in its pleasant places…*'

Washington Irving

'*If you live without any kind of self-reflection, the days fly by and before you know it, your time here is finished.*'

Seon Master Daehang

CHAPTER EIGHT:

KING MURYONG'S TOMB

For the first several centuries AD, three Korean dynasties competed for power — Koguryo, Paekche and Shilla. King Muryong, or Muryongwang, ascended the throne of the Paekche Kingdom, which had its capital in Kongju, after his father was assassinated in the year 501. The building of King Muryong's tomb began twenty years later while he was still alive. Quite the memento mori. Constructed of black bricks with lotus-flower designs, it was given a vaulted chamber with niches for oil lamps, and a low, narrow entrance to be guarded by a stone animal figure. It was built inside the slope of a hill, after the tombs of Liang China.

The Paekche Kingdom built good relations with Japan, with Paekche architects exporting their temple-building skills to the neighbouring country. Muryongwang ruled the Paekche Kingdom for twenty-three years, and was laid in the tomb three years after his death. His coffin was made from three-hundred-year-old pine trees imported from Japan. His wife died a year later, and she eventually joined her husband, and the entrance to the tomb was closed up with bricks. The Paekche capital, which had been at Kongju for only fifty years, was transferred elsewhere, and Kongju's brief spell of importance was over.

The express bus terminal was modern, enormous and splendid, but when I asked the girl behind the ticket counter in my best Korean if there was a bus, *bosu*, to Kongju, she smiled in embarrassment, giggled, said something to her colleague, and tried her best to ignore me. Because I didn't go away, she finally did summon assistance, in the form of a young man who spoke English and explained I was in the Honam Terminal, and but should be in the Kyongbu Terminal. Such was the Seoul-style humiliation of the beginning of my first trip into the country.

The other bus station was attached to this one but accessed via a complex route of escalators and arcades, and the kind young man took me there so I wouldn't get lost. Other men volunteered help as soon as they saw me with backpack and guidebook, even though they often didn't know much more than I did. Possibly offering assistance was simply the done thing, even if you didn't have a clue. Saving face and all that. I finally spotted a 'Foreigners' ticket office, where I discovered I'd been mixing up my Kongju with my Keongju, or maybe my Kungju. Those pesky names.

The bus to Kongju left on time, barely half-full, which was pleasant – the joys of travelling off-peak, the sheer luxury of a long bus journey and the space and quiet to read a book while glancing up at the landscape passing by, the start of an adventure. Eventually we escaped the thick of the city and were on the highway surrounded by open country with forest-covered mountains in the distance, though occasionally the landscape was still scattered with faceless, numbered apartment towers. I slept for a while and woke to another world of farmland, fields and greenhouses. In flat rice paddies, blue sky was reflected in the water between the rows of bright green shoots. A lone figure in baggy clothes and wide-brimmed straw hat stood knee-deep in water. White long-billed egrets or herons picked at the crops. Shallow rivers wound through valleys.

We stopped for people to stretch, or squat down and smoke and spit, and some of the older passengers stared at me. When we boarded again, a friendly, curious old man in a brightly patterned Hawaiian-style shirt sitting behind me asked where I was going, and did I live in Kongju? No, I told him, and, grateful for the interest, explained as well as I could about staying in Seoul. He thanked me politely, then turned back to his friends and spent the rest of the journey telling an interminable yarn, the most emotional parts punctuated by a throaty *khkhh* sound that sounded like radio interference.

We arrived at Kongju, which according to the very informative ticket was 131.8 kilometres from Seoul, at 7 p.m. Declining the services of an insistent taxi driver, I shouldered my backpack and wandered off to get my bearings by finding the river. And there it was, immense and spectacular, with rippling currents, stretching off into the hills. I walked down to the banks, where people were jogging. The sun was setting and there were plentiful midges and dragonflies. The wide expanse of water crashed thunderously over the weir.

I walked back up to the bridge and sauntered across in the direction of town. Stopping to take photos, I saw an old man with a friendly face and an amputated hand limping slowly in my direction, with the help of a rather spotty younger man. The old man greeted me and asked where I was from, and then said, 'Beautiful', which I decided must surely refer to where I was from, and not me, despite the way he seemed to look at me when he said it.

'Why Kongju?' he asked. I pointed to the view, the sun setting behind a distant mountain, the vast, gleaming, pale river flowing towards it, hoping this illustrated my reasons for being here well enough. 'Kumgang,' he noted, the name of the river, and then pointed upriver: 'Puyo – eighty kilometres.' I nodded. He then ventured, 'Puyo – forty kilometres,' as if I had challenged this outrageous claim of eighty kilometres. Or maybe he was just talking about another place that sounded like Puyo, and I couldn't hear the difference.

He asked where I was eating and sleeping. Vaguely suspicious of the expression on his face – sweet old men being not always what they seem to be – I smiled, feigned incomprehension, apologised and said goodbye. The old man continued his arduous walk, but then his young companion with the bad skin came back. I thought perhaps he wanted to explain something about the old man.

'God is love,' he said. 'Jesus Christ? God is love.'

I nodded.

'Hallelujah,' he added, smiled and walked on.

The sun had sunk below the hills, and in the fading light I watched a lone silhouetted figure bent over the mudflats, maybe fishing.

Walking into town, I realised that, unlike in Seoul, here I presented a figure of amusing novelty. My mere presence in Kongju elicited a few surprised smiles, which I liked. The street signs for some reason were in the Roman alphabet, so it was easy enough to find my way about. Women zipped around town on mopeds. The air was noticeably fresher here. When I opened the door of a pleasant-looking *yogwan*, a couple were sitting on the floor eating dinner. They agreed to let me have a comfortable, spotless room with private bath and western bed for 20,000 won. I deposited my bag in the room then rushed out again.

My first trip alone felt good. I'd already met people. Not much of a city gal, I wanted to get outdoors, start stretching my limbs and feeling the sun on my skin. I also needed to learn something. My brain had started turning to mush in sometimes soul-less Seoul. Just to show he was happy for me to travel on my own, Gav had treated me to a fantastic lunch at the Hyatt of seafood salad and tiramisu before I set off. What a man. I managed to find a telephone attached to a 'Coffee and Can' vending machine on the main street and send him my love before he headed to work.

After wandering around the small town centre I found a place to sit and write my first impressions of beyond the city limits of Seoul. The 'ye olde' lanterns outside the restaurant and the traditional wooden booths inside belied what was actually a merrily buzzing young people's bar, where they served ice-cold *hof* with a sizzling sweetcorn snack and squeezy-bottle mayonnaise. I spent an hour there and then walked some more, but by ten o'clock Kongju seemed to be closing down for the night. The only people around were shopkeepers cleaning up or wearily eating supper, and I heard frogs croaking down by the canal. There were a few upstairs lounges, but they looked unpromising, and I made my way towards the *yogwan* and my book, not really unhappy that I wasn't, for once, staying up until two or three in the morning.

Then, across the road I noticed a neon sign – 'Lee Ga Salon' – with a few people milling beneath it. Since I wasn't yet the slightest bit tired I looked inside the doorway that led down stairs, assuming it was a bar where I might meet some locals. On closer inspection it looked more like a health club. All I could see was a smart counter and doors off down a corridor. I was turning back to cross the street when a plumpish young man smoking a cigarette invited me to come back inside and see the 'house'. What was I doing...? There was only one way to find out.

Nervously I followed him to the bottom of the stairs, where someone came out from behind the reception desk and guided us down a bare hallway. He opened a numbered door – yikes! – onto a small dark room, where couches curved around a table laden with food and bottles. *Annyung haseyo!* A young couple and a young woman, probably my new friend's girlfriend, greeted me and one of them poured me a shot of brandy as I sat down. Glancing around, I noticed a large television on the wall by the door: on the screen, oiled-up girls wrestled in leather bikinis. Eek, what? But then I saw the microphones and the song book. I was in nothing more sinister than a 'singing room' or *norae bang*, a private Korean karaoke room.

These were hugely popular, I knew, but I'd never seen one. I have never been able to hold a note, as my poor music teachers would attest, and although it doesn't stop me singing to myself when walking down the street, karaoke has never appealed. Besides, the couples in this room were very young, and though they were clearly impressed their friend had found a foreigner outside, I was spoiling their fun. They were on their best behaviour for me. We stumbled through some belaboured small talk in English and Korean until I finished the brandy, thanked them and left. My host gave me his business card – he worked in a photo studio – and said he would drive me around Kongju tomorrow if I called.

I'd done much better meeting people here than on a typical night in Seoul, even if it had been a bit surprising. When I got back to the *yogwan*, the owners were sleeping on the floor, she with her head on a soft pillow, he with a hard rectangular block, and I had to wake them to get my key. Aromatic coils burned in the hallways to keep the little flies at bay. I was pleased to go to sleep early for a change. There was much I wanted to see the next day.

In 1971, more than fourteen centuries after the death of Paekche King Muryong, while drainage work was carried out on a burial hill just outside Kongju, someone discovered King Muryong's tomb. Unlike the other mausolems on the hill, which had been mostly looted during invasions, this one was untouched and absolutely intact. Inside were two lacquered wooden coffins with bronze handles and almost three thousand burial objects, many of them pieces of jewellery. A tablet in the entrance to the tomb gave the details of the king and queen who inhabited it and the exact date when King Muryong 'bought' this plot from the God of Land. From this one discovery, experts had been able to date all excavated objects surviving from the Paekche Dynasty. It was this tomb that had drawn me to Kongju.

I made my way up to the archaeological park with some difficulty. It was very hot and humid, as usual, and the flying bugs were annoying. I'd already spent the morning wandering around the town's old fortress, and it was a fair walk out of town to the park's entrance, so I was bright red in the face by the time I arrived. The young woman at the information desk was extremely welcoming, however, and asked me to come back and see her on my way out as she wanted some help with her 'English composition'.

On a green hillside, I found the replica of King Muryong's tomb, vivid and spooky. Photographs showed the archaeological find as it was when they first entered the tomb. The objects found inside the vault included the king's heavy gold and jade earrings and hairpins, and gold diadems with each arm like a blossoming branch; ornamental shoes; a bronze mirror with a swallow-tail; bowls and coins, spoons and chopsticks; a glass figurine and beads; and a wooden head-rest with phoenix ornamentation and wooden foot-rests decorated with trees. And there was the stone tablet, with the epitaph 'The Great General of Pacifying the East' inscribed in Chinese characters, because this was before the days of the Korean alphabet.

I walked farther up the hill to find the doorways to the actual tombs, but all of course were closed and roped off. Some had cables leading in, and I remembered reading that they had to keep the temperature and humidity regulated to stop further decay, which is why they had created a replica for visitors. Apparently the paintings of tomb number 6 – of a blue dragon, a white tiger, a black turtle and snake, and a red phoenix – were being discoloured by exposure to the air. Captivated by the story and the atmosphere of the place, so deeply tied to the early history of Korea, I was tantalised by what hid behind those unguarded doors. But there was nothing to be done, so I walked up the hill to see more of the park and enjoy the trees and peaceful grassy slopes.

When, half an hour later, I followed the path back down to the mounds, some of the doors were open, and a man with a truck was working on the cables. I had no idea which was the entrance to King Muryong's tomb, but I hovered, wondering if I could possibly sneak a look around the man as he worked. Eventually he motioned me over to the entranceway into the hillside. Had he read my mind? He gestured to me to follow him carefully.

We crept along a damp stone tunnel into the hill itself, knelt down in the dust to crawl through a tiny entranceway, and – holding my breath – I stood up inside King Muryong's tomb. In the light from the workman's torch I could make out the bluish-black brick walls all around me, the same ones that had kept King Muryong and his wife and belongings safe from marauding Japanese and Chinese and other plunderers for so many centuries. There were the niches for lamps but other than that, it was empty. Why the man had chosen to invite me inside, I didn't know – but with this small gesture I felt my relationship with Korea had changed. An act of kindness, an intimate brush with Korea's ancient history. It was an almost spiritual moment.

As I wandered down the hill in a kind of daze, three cleaning ladies in colourful baggy clothes, with brightly coloured sun visors strapped around their foreheads, stopped their work and shouted, '*Annyung haseyo!*' A tiny woman came up and gave me to understand I had a nice face. '*Kamsamnida,*' I said and smiled. She asked how old I was and seemed surprised by my answer of *sam-ship*, or thirty, presumably because I was dressed like a scruffy teenager in shorts and a black vest and trainers, not at all lady-like. She told me she was fifty-nine. I hadn't yet figured out why it was important to exchange ages, so I wasn't really sure what to say. She asked was I *honja*, alone? Yes, *honja*. We all smiled at one another and waved goodbye.

I returned to the information desk at the entrance. The young woman who'd asked me to come back now sat me down and fetched coffee, telling me in English some interesting information about the site and the treasures. Apparently the niches in the walls had held six white porcelain bowls, now in the museum, which were older than even the first examples of Chinese white glazed porcelain. Then she brought out some papers – she was making up a sign for visitors, and wanted some help with the English. She was very sweet and we laughed as we tried to figure out what it was exactly she wanted to say. And so it was I helped her figure out how best to write that, to protect the ancient site, the original tomb of King Muryong was permanently closed to visitors. While the new replica was being built, visitors were invited to watch the video in the information centre. I casually, guiltily brushed some dust off my knees.

After, still elated, I walked back into town to the market that backed onto the canal. Washing hung out to dry from wooden and corrugated-iron shacks leaning over the water, dilapidated but seedily picturesque, so unlike the modern look of Seoul. The market itself was a wonderful maze, with whole stalls of different noodles and ginseng, fish packed in boxes with coils burning sweet smoke to keep the flies off, hot twisted doughnuts fresh from the pan. The alleys were covered with tarpaulins and finely woven nets to keep out sun and rain. A frail old woman was smoking a cigarette through a bamboo pipe. Noticing pretty, aproned women carrying trays filled with bowls of soup and stews on their heads, I remembered I hadn't eaten. From a tiny eatery a well-dressed woman in her fifties holding a fan beckoned me to join her.

Conversation was more or less limited to place names, places she'd visited that I knew: San Fran-cis-co! Nia-ga-ra! But she ordered food for me and showed me how to eat it. We got large bowls filled with steamed rice and barley, mixed with chopped cucumber and hot red sauce. From an assortment of bowls we added steamed greens, beansprouts, chopped carrot, and mild kimchi made with something like spinach. We mixed in a soupy sauce and ate it with a spoon, accompanied by cold tea. Delicious. On my way back out of the market, I couldn't resist buying some freshly made twisted doughnuts for later.

Grinning schoolkids leaned out of bus windows to shout hello in English as I emerged at last onto the street. There had been a few Seoul-style blank stares and sniffs in Kongju, but this had been a wonderful adventure. And I still had another couple of days before I was due back in Seoul for the weekend.

CHAPTER NINE:

THE PATH TO BUDDHA

Buddhism, founded by Prince Siddhartha Gautama in what is now Nepal around five centuries BC, first made its way to Korea from China in the fourth century AD. Encouraged by the Koguryo Kingdom, one of those early Three Kingdoms, it had a profound impact. A distinctive Korean Buddhism developed, and then was passed on to Japan. In 533 the king of Paekche (Muryong's successor) sent a statue of Buddha to Japan and recommended Buddhism as the basis for a happy life, and Paekche architects built temples in Japan.

The teachings of the enlightened one stress self-knowledge, self-discipline and loving kindness as the way to perfect peace. Buddhism thrived in Korea, deeply affecting thought and culture. It was the state religion throughout the next dynasty, Koryo – the dynasty that gave us our name for Korea, meaning 'high mountains and *sparkling waters', and which lasted from the tenth to the fourteenth century, the equivalent of Europe's Middle Ages. Buddhist monks held high positions as advisors to the monarch.*

But after the Koryo Dynasty was overthrown, the new Choson Dynasty, based in Seoul, gradually began a regime of reform. Although in its early days there were fervent Buddhists such as King Sejong, Confucian doctrine became the moral foundation of the Choson Dynasty. In an effort to rid the country of Buddhist influence, Confucians drove monks and their temples into the hills, barring religious leaders from interfering in state affairs. Buddhism survived in isolated mountain places, however, endured, and today is thriving again.

Yesan seemed a pretty useless place to go, according to my Lonely Planet guidebook. But when the woman at the ticket desk in Kongju said it wasn't possible to go to Kapsa, where I'd planned to go, I took the bus to Yesan. From Yesan I could take another bus to Toksan, and from there I could get to a Buddhist monastery called Sudoksa.

By early evening I was standing under a shop's awning in the town of Toksan in the pouring rain, trying to figure out where to spend the night, and how to avoid being drenched to the skin. I had my tent in my backpack and would prefer to camp to save money, since all I wanted was to sleep, but it really was pouring down. Rainy season had started in earnest, it seemed. It was too late to get to the monastery, but I hoped I'd be able to find a bus there in the morning. Then a car stopped, the window rolled down and a fine-featured man with a smooth head and soft, voluminous, grey monk's robes asked:

'*Odi gan?*'

Where was I going? 'Sudoksa,' I said, wondering if he'd advise me on how to find it or something. But no, it appeared from his gesture that he was offering me a lift.

'*Kamsamnida,*' I said, thanking him, and got in.

I tried to cover my bare legs with my backpack. Of course I had to be wearing my shortest hiking shorts. As we made our way slowly through sheets of rain in the air-conditioned car, he tried to make conversation, but neither of us had enough of the other's language. Eventually, he found some classical music on the digital dial, then put in the earpiece of his mobile phone to check his messages.

After driving for ten minutes or so, we passed through a gate, and halfway up a forested mountain arrived at the monastery under darkening skies. Imposing buildings in traditional style rose from the hillside at intervals: long, black-tiled roofs, the eaves painted in delicate pinks and greens, decorated with flower and animal carvings; sturdy red wooden pillars, delicate trellised doors with paper windows. They looked like the palaces in Seoul, except surrounded by woods. Though there is no historical record, historians believe there has been a temple here on the mountain at Toksan since 599, and the worshippers practised Seon, or Zen Buddhism. We stopped and the monk disappeared into one of the halls, asking me to wait.

I watched the mist rise from the trees and glanced onto the backseat, spying a football and a brochure for 'Travelling in Malaysia'. I couldn't help thinking the monk was going to emerge embarrassed, having discovered I had no invitation, no right to be here.

Instead, he invited me into what turned out to be a canteen, and asked if I wanted to eat. When I said I wasn't hungry, a boy of about twelve gave me an umbrella and two monks led me across the sandy courtyard, skirting puddles, past a stone pagoda and towards the Hall of the White Lotus. Instead of passing by, we walked up steps to a raised walkway kept dry under the long eaves – aha! Now the shape of the roofs made sense. Sliding wooden doors were drawn open on a bright, bare room. I left my shoes outside as was customary and from behind more sliding doors the monks brought out pretty satin cushioned quilts and a pink, seed-filled pillow, and I was left alone with a bow and a smile.

Incredulous, I spent the evening sequestered in that perfect, simple space, listening to thunder in the hills and the ceaseless splashing and crashing of the rain as it poured off the eaves. Opening my wood-and-paper shutters, which were held back by carved wooden turtles, I looked out into the semi-dark and smelled the fresh air. Lightning floodlit the courtyard from time to time, revealing gnarled trees and, sheltered by a wooden pavilion, a giant iron bell and a hanging log in the shape of a fish. Monks ran around in robes and slippers, carrying umbrellas, avoiding the pooling water. The two who'd brought me here returned a couple of times, once to give me a candle when the storm was too bad to have the electric light on, and again to check I was comfortable. 'Breakfast is at eight,' they said, then conferred. Wrong word? 'No, sorry, six.' Smiles, bows.

Because of the unfamiliar routine, I found myself lying wide awake at midnight and in a dead sleep by the morning. It was my first time with seed-filled pillows and quilts on the floor, but at least I was warm and dry. For someone who has always liked sitting on the floor, it's an easy enough step to sleeping on one. We've all done it at people's houses after parties.

Thanks to my alarm clock, I made it blearily to breakfast, having splashed myself down with cold water in the washroom. In the canteen a monk in brown robes mutely helped fill my steel tray with rice, boiled greens, fresh beansprouts, tofu and mushroom soup, roasted potatoes and kimchi, all of which were delicious. Breakfast was quiet. Six tiny boys with cropped hair, in T-shirts and shorts, sleepy-eyed but with different expressions like six of the seven dwarfs, were guided to sit near me at the long table. They were 'child monks', aged four and five, I was told, training to be monks. One looked especially tired and grumpy, and a middle-aged lady gave them 1,000-won notes to cheer them up.

So there I was, in a traditional, working Korean Buddhist monastery in the early morning. It was peaceful after the storm, and a fog hung close to the hillside, but it somehow felt lighter and more dewy than any I'd felt before in Seoul. A monk swept a courtyard, but everyone else had disappeared, leaving the place empty, so I ventured to explore. The main temple was a simple wooden structure, with a tall ceiling and plain wooden floor. Its graceful architecture bore signs of the influence of the Paekche Dynasty, of which King Muryong was a part, a sign of the venerable age of this

Buddhist site. A hidden inscription on the main beam in the temple apparently said it was completed in 1308, 'the thirty-fourth year of King Chungnyol'. Few wooden structures had survived that long in Korea, thanks to repeated invasions and the war. Most were burned down and rebuilt again and again.

Five golden statues faced benignly through the open front wall out across the valley, three of them representing the past, present and future Buddha. Hanging paintings – paper or cloth, unframed and unmounted – lined the walls with stylised but lively, intensely detailed scenes of gods and kings. On the roof beams were faint centuries-old dragon paintings.

Finding it was still only 7 a.m., I took a path up the moist hillside, vaguely following the tocking of a wooden instrument. Steps led into forest beside a stream cascading over boulders just as I'd seen in paintings in the temple. Several groups of monks passed me on their way down, smiled happily and wished me a good day. One asked cheerily,

'Where are you going?'

I grinned and shrugged. 'Up the mountain!'

He laughed, and pointed up the steps: 'Only two minutes! See you again!'

I continued, and fifteen thigh-tightening minutes later realised the monk had a wicked sense of humour.

I'd reached the top of the steps when I found a thatched house. An inscription on the rock said it was the hermitage of Mangong, a Seon master who lived here in the early twentieth century and helped revive the Buddhist tradition in Korea. During the Japanese occupation, monks who didn't agree to support the occupiers had simply disappeared.

With the repression of Buddhism by the Confucian Choson Dynasty, and all the burning down of temples by the Japanese invaders, monks seem to have had a tough calling. Christianity, which arrived in Korea in the eighteenth century, has grown in popularity, particularly during Korea's recent economic boom. But a quarter of South Koreans call themselves Buddhists, and people are often Confucianists, Buddhists and Christians at the same time.

As I turned away from the hermitage, I realised the path continued straight up. Although it was tough walking that steep path in the growing heat and humidity, and views down the valley were obscured by clouds, the forest was peaceful: just rocks, short bushy pine trees, whistling birds, and mist blown along on a faint breeze. I continued up. There were mounds of pebbles by the stream, and slabs of rock for bridges, and little messages I couldn't understand on flags hanging from the tree branches over the path. Then suddenly, the path turned into a clearing and revealed the most beautiful statue I had ever seen, standing in the mist, against a cliff of pink rock that had been crept over by moss and ivy. The Buddha stood the height of two men, holding a vial, with an expression of absolute serenity. Candles and flowers and brass bowls had been laid at the statue's feet. Across the clearing was a spring beside tall bamboo. The trees around held still the moist air, and the mist enclosed the whole scene – nothing could be seen beyond. The only sounds were of birds and water.

Back at the monastery, I met a cheerful woman with short black hair and gold-rimmed glasses and a pretty laugh. Her grey clothes made me think she might be a nun.

'I am Kim Moon-sim,' she said, smiling and adjusting her glasses, 'and I am curator of Sudoksa Museum.' Koreans give their family name first, and because Kim is such a popular family name (almost half of South Koreans are called Kim, Lee or Park), they have two given names, hyphenated together. She spoke English, and told me she would show me around. I was being assigned my own guide. The museum opened here in 1999 to promote an understanding of Buddhism and protect the treasures, inspired by the life and practice of the two great Seon masters who lived here. It was created with the help of the Korean government and Askadera, the oldest such temple in Japan. Most visitors were Korean, Japanese or Chinese Buddhists on pilgrimages.

Taking me into the museum, Kim Moon-sim pointed out the displays showing bowls that once belonged to Seon masters, and their rag robes for winter and wooden slippers for wet weather. The eighteenth- and nineteenth-century originals of the hanging paintings from the temple were in glass cases here. Feeling I should find out more about the treasures, I asked about what looked like two tiny pieces of grey stone in a box on display.

'They are, um, relics,' she said. She looked something up in her pocket dictionary and confirmed. 'Yes, relics.' Bones, perhaps, I speculated?

I tried asking about another object on display, this time pointing to a holy book. With momentarily furrowed brow, Miss Kim flipped through a dictionary. Then she consulted Chung-am, a monk with cropped black hair and a tan complexion, dressed in loose voluminous grey robes and slippers, who'd come to join us. He spoke to her in Korean for what seemed a long time then he threw up his hands with a laugh, eyes sparkling, and went to play on the multimedia screen instead.

'Sorry!' I laughed. 'It's OK.' It was a little too complex to explain to a neophyte, I suspected. A non-Buddhist western woman arriving alone, wearing short shorts and a tight T-shirt was an oddity here to say the least, yet I'd met with nothing but smiling kindness. As we left the museum, I tried to buy postcards as a thank you, but they wouldn't accept any money. A softly spoken man in secular clothes invited me to sign the guest book, and followed us across to the canteen for lunch. When we'd been up to the counter to fill our trays and sat down at the long tables, he asked me where I was from.

'I've come here from Canada,' I said, 'but I'm originally from England.'

'Are there many Buddhist temples in Canada?' he asked.

'Er, no, I don't think so.' Certainly not like this, I thought.

Meanwhile, Miss Kim had a laugh over my clumsy use of chopsticks, and we bonded over my need for guidance with basic eating.

Other visitors were milling about or heading up the mountain by the afternoon, when Miss Kim took me on a walk around the monastery. The 1,080 steps I had taken up the mountain that morning, she told me, were related to the path to enlightenment. She took me to the temple and showed me what to do when entering, how to kneel before the Buddha, and how to show respect to the monks by putting my hands together and bowing. I bowed to the lady who looked after the temple, too, and she smiled and said, 'Have a lucky day!' I met a lady in a wide-brimmed straw hat who let visitors buy prayer tiles, and Chung-am and Kim Moon-sim pressed gifts on me. To show my gratitude I tried to buy some keepsakes, including a wooden bead bracelet, but again they wouldn't let me pay, and apparently I couldn't pay for my room and board either because this was a Buddhist place. These funny, charming, calm people had been so generous and welcoming, I really didn't want to go back to Seoul. These few days in the countryside had opened up Korea for me as a place with an enchanting spirit.

When it was time to leave, Chung-am insisted on driving me to town in one of the communal monk-cars. On either side of the road, bright green rice fields descended in tiers from hillsides he told me were named after phoenix and dragons. When we got to Hongsong, he insisted on buying my bus ticket back to Seoul, then said goodbye. I walked around Hongsong for an hour in a light-headed state of confusion before I could bring myself to get on a bus.

Later I tried to find out about the 'child monks' I had seen at the monastery. Monasteries have for centuries taken in small boys to receive a religious education, while giving them the freedom to leave if they choose not to become monks. I read online about a programme at another South Korean monastery, Haeinsa. Most of the thirty-seven child monks there had been abandoned by parents who were divorced or too poor or too young to care for them. More than ninety per cent had been physically abused before being left at the temple. Buddhists say these children were monks in their past lives, and hardship at a young age is necessary to lead them back to the path. But they attend a local school and will make their own decision as to whether they want to become monks. Local volunteers cook the meals and wash their clothes. Muhak, the monk who started that programme, says he refuses to accept children at the parents' first request, as it's not simply an orphanage. 'This is the house of mercy where we cultivate souls.'

CHAPTER TEN:

HEART AND SEOUL

'Hey babe,' said Gav, welcoming me back with a big hug.

Still dreamy over the last few days, somehow I managed to explain everything that had happened.

'I feel bad that you weren't there,' I said.

'No, I'm happy for you!' He said. But I could tell he wished he'd been there. Although I didn't say it, I felt different after what I'd experienced. A whole new Korea had opened up for me. All the way on the bus back to Seoul, I wrote in my notebook about the monastery. Or, I should say, the story wrote itself. And now I was excited about sharing it with people.

Although it had been years since I'd done any journalism, having put all that aside once I started working as an agent, I was encouraged enough by this to make an appointment to visit the English-language *Korea Herald* offices and speak to the editor about writing occasionally for the paper's weekend supplement. I also made contact with a paper back home. This was a profoundly important summer to be in Korea, with the historic summit in June and the symbolic reuniting of certain families planned for August. But I'd never been good at news and current affairs, at thinking of what the person on the street wants to know. I wanted to discover the secret places that spoke to me of Korea's culture. Writing would challenge me to explore and think about them. I had this opportunity to follow a new path of learning, and the freedom of a journey dictated by no itinerary.

Life went on as usual in Seoul, and laundry needed to be done: from the sublime to the ridiculous. But I discovered a new laundry place on our hill which, prosaic as it was, made me happy. Perhaps I was becoming more Buddhist. Laundry places weren't self-service – you brought your bags of clothes to be washed and dried. The place we had used before was a designated 'Foreigners Laundry' near the Hyatt, but there the people had no great prowess in English, and this local one was cheaper and better. The pleasant, smart young man who ran it (and I was impressed to find a young man running a laundry) now recognised me, so the transaction was easy. I gave him the bags with the colours separated from the whites, he gestured he'd wash them separately. I asked in a rudimentary fashion – *'Naeil?'* – if I could pick them up the next day.

'Tomorrow evening,' he responded in English.

And I replied in Korean, *'Kamsamnida!'* And sure enough, they were all clean and neatly folded as promised the next evening, and I lugged them up the steep hill to our apartment, pleased that I'd been allowed to do some non-foreign laundry.

My Korean was coming along slowly, and the few days in the country where I got to speak to people had helped my confidence. Single words like *naeil* were easy enough to master. But sentences seemed infinitely more complicated, words suddenly sprouting polite suffixes like *-ssumnida* and extra little words I didn't know all over the place. And something as common as 'goodbye' appeared to assume different forms. I'd heard *annyung kyeseyo* and *annyunghi kasipsiyo*, not to be confused with *annyung haseyo*, which is hello. Though there was also *annyunghi jumuseyo*. Yikes. But most of these seemed to work OK. The sounds of Korean were difficult to reproduce in the Roman alphabet, so it wasn't always clear how to pronounce things. But I tried to listen.

My laptop computer had stopped working, and I couldn't tell if it was because I used the wrong adaptor and caused a power surge or just that, since I bought it second-hand a couple of years ago, it had chosen this moment to die. Thankfully I was in the right country to have a computer problem, and the young man behind the desk at the computer room Click gave me the contact details for a computer doctor, Sean Kim. He spoke good English as he had lived in Australia, presumably why he called himself Sean Kim instead of Kim Sean-something, and he arrived wearing a Roots Canada T-shirt. A computer doctor who did house calls! He and his friend took their shoes off at the door. I told them they didn't need to, but they felt uncomfortable not doing so, even in a westerner's flat, as it wasn't 'Korean style'. Koreans sit and sleep on the floor, so they always remove their shoes before entering a house.

'You are an English teacher?' Sean Kim asked me.

'No, I'm here because my boyfriend is a drummer and works in the Hyatt Hotel, at JJ's.'

'Ahhh!' Sean translated for his friend and they both voiced approval. 'Nice place!'

Sean was friendly and I enjoyed meeting a Korean in Seoul I could actually talk to.

He told me Koreans were scared of foreigners because most Koreans didn't speak English, and therefore didn't know how to communicate. In the main, only older Koreans, who learned English from American soldiers during the war, spoke the language with confidence. Americans had remained here since the war broke out, though, so it seemed odd to me that so few Koreans picked up the language. I supposed there hadn't been much contact. I thought again of the beer labels in English ('Health! Fresh!'); was it for the Americans, or was it trendy? English was taught in schools now, but I expected it would be grammar-based with few opportunities to practice speaking. I'd have thought English would be more popular, as the language of international commerce.

Still, perhaps because I was happier and smiling more this week, I'd noticed more people smiling back at me, and when that happened it always made my day.

Gav and I browsed the shops along Itaewonno, where the salespeople spoke English and there were signs advertising custom-made suits for bargain prices. When Gav tried on a black leather jacket, the salesman desperately tried to convince him that it fit by pulling on the shoulders and sleeves.

'Very nice!'

'No, it doesn't fit,' said Gav, who had a pretty good idea of when a jacket hung properly and when it didn't. He worked in a suit shop one summer and was surprised how many customers, especially the shorter and stockier ones, tried to convince themselves something fitted when it looked dreadful. 'Have you got it in a larger size?'

The man pulled out a jacket in a completely different shape and colour, and handed it to him, seemingly baffled when Gav said he wasn't actually interested in a red blouson-style alternative.

In the evening, I went down to the posh end of Itaewonno again, and found another lovely coffee shop called 'Chocolate'. It had taken the idea of comfort to kitsch extreme, with loveseats and glass tables, pretty lights, French ballads and Spanish serenades playing through the speakers. My hot chocolate came with whipped cream in a mug, and an artsy handmade folder for the bill. It cost the same as a bus ticket to Kongju or a meal, but hey, I deserved it. The waiters were all smiles, and mine was sporting short cycling shorts, an ankle-length black apron and 'long shoes' with square toes and buckles reminiscent of renaissance courtiers. He was rather well built and somehow didn't look ridiculous, or at least no more ridiculous than the average runway model.

I probably cut a strange figure here myself in my extra-short green shorts (Abercrombie and Fitch, made in Korea, bought from a stall in Itaewon), army T-shirt (genuine US army article, from Namdaemun Market), rugged black running shoes (Timberland, bought in Canada, undoubtedly the most useful item I brought), and black army shoulder bag. Maybe people in Seoul thought I was with the army. I'd taken to wearing my hair in a ponytail to stay cool; it got so wavy with the humidity that it was easier that way. It was a brutalist look, but I felt in better shape after getting some exercise and fresh air and sunshine during my trip into the countryside, so I didn't feel nearly as awkward as a month ago.

People in Seoul took great pride in their appearance — even if the effect was unusual. Lots of young Korean men liked to dye their hair bright primary colours. One I saw had dyed his hair the same striking royal blue as his suit. Generally men wore loose casual trousers and shirts, but that day on the edge of Namsan Park I'd seen a bent old man with a white billy-goat beard wearing a light fedora and a beautiful white *hanbok*, the traditional pyjama-like suit, the jacket crossed in front in a V like a martial arts jacket and tied with ribbons at the side. His baggy trousers were tucked into his socks, which some men seemed to favour, perhaps as a precaution against mosquitoes bites?

One afternoon we went to Myungdong, one of the city's most youthful districts, devoted to fashion and cosmetics. We wandered hand in hand around streets filled with crowds of teenagers buying eyeliners and hair gel, loud music blasting in every direction. The three-storey Starbucks was the biggest in Asia when it was first built. Doll-like girls in space-warrior outfits and leg-warmers promoted cell phones outside. Did anyone in Seoul still not have one?

A handful of Myungdong's streets were lined with cheap, cheerful cafes. Ladies sat in the window wearing aprons and plastic gloves, making Korean snack sushi, *kimbap*. They scooped a spoonful of *bap*, rice, and layered it onto a paper-thin black square of *kim*, seaweed, adding strips of luncheon meat or tinned tuna, pickled radish, cucumber or steamed greens, or kimchi; then rolled it up tightly into a fat sausage using a slatted wooden mat, sprinkled it with sesame seeds, and sliced it into bite-sized circles. I asked Gav if he was up for going inside, and he was all for it.

Inside, the menus and walls featured photos of the colourful food: red sauce, green leaves, bright orange carrot, white rice. A plastic jug of ice-cold water was brought to our table and eventually one of the waitresses overcame her embarrassed giggles enough to take our order. It was steamy in the cafe, smelling of garlic and soybean paste, and noisy with slurping and chattering and people shouting *Yogio!* for the waiter to come, and waiters shouting hello, *annyung haseyo!* or goodbye, *annyung kyeseyo! Kimbap* was eaten with chopsticks and a side helping of hot broth delicately seasoned with green onion or seaweed. *Mandu* were sweet pork dumplings served with soy sauce. Stews bubbled in black earthenware bowls that retained the heat of the oven. *Dolsot bibimbap* kept cooking as you ate, leaving lovely crispy bits to be scraped off the bowl. Noodles came with fresh cabbage, carrot, cucumber and beansprouts, mixed with hot sauce, *bibim naengmyun*. This type of Korean food was wholesome, satisfying, unrefined but rough and crunchy and chewy, all buckwheat noodles and barley rice, and everything was priced very reasonably between 2,000 and 4,000 won.

On other days in central Seoul we battled thousands of umbrellas thrown up against the rainy season. It rained for twelve hours one night, and was still pouring when I woke up, in the dark, to the sounds of lovemaking. Neighbours left their window open. The air was cool and fresh in the morning, the streets a little cleaner, and that afternoon the sun came out while I was reading and sitting cross-legged on a wooden bench in Namsan Park. How civilised that taking off your shoes in public was considered good form. That night the sky was clear enough to show some stars – I'd never noticed them in Seoul before. It even felt refreshingly cool when I finished my writing session at Click. I'd taken to writing there since the laptop stopped functioning. It was more atmospheric, anyway.

Tokjokdo, one of about three thousand rocky islands around Korea's coasts, is in the Yellow or West Sea between Korea and China. Nearly eighty kilometres from the mainland, it was an hour-long, high-speed ferry ride from Inchon. We were off to the island for what we hoped would be a romantic Sunday together. Through the window we saw the craggy rocks of islands, Tokjokdo's coastline dotted with coves.

We arrived to a glorious, blue-skied afternoon and an empty kilometre or so of fine sand, a perfect arc of white shelving gently down into shallow waves. The backdrop of low hills was covered with an uninterrupted blanket of green forest. Fishing boats bobbed at anchor as we walked around the bay. There was little to do except watch the crabs scuttle into their holes in the sand as you sipped a cold *maekju* and prepared yourself for diving into clean, salty water. The tide was out and the water balmy.

When you've been cooped up in a city for days, the body hunched and slumped, what a pleasure to stretch out the limbs in the sun, glide through saltwater, tighten the muscles and breathe deeply. We spent a couple of hours messing around on the beach, then put up our tent on a pristine stretch of sand, with only the seagulls for company. It was good to get away together. Gav looked lovely with a bit of sun on his face, sand in his ruffled golden hair, combat pants rolled up to his knees.

The village was set back some way from the beach and hidden behind pine trees. There were upmarket guesthouses and a few restaurants, but most people had set up picnic mats on the beach and were quietly enjoying the cool evening air and the sound of the waves. After the expensive ferry ride we didn't need an expensive dinner – we were happy to eat *kyeran ramyun*, spicy instant noodles with an egg cracked into them.

As we settled into the tent later, some men came by and asked us to move. We were disappointed: this seemed so perfect. It turned out, however, they were only asking that we move up the beach to avoid being washed away by the incoming tide, plus a mere 1,000 won for camping fees and use of the shower-*jang*. We enjoyed a calm night. Clouds obscured most of the stars, but it was easy to imagine what a wonderful sky you might see otherwise. Lights revealed one or two fishing boats out at sea.

In the morning, fog rolled in so heavily we could barely see the hills, though the sun was hot. Women were walking down the shoreline picking up seaweed, as we saw them the night before picking shellfish from the sand – both would go in a noodle soup or stew, mostly likely. A wizened old lady came by and sold us hot corn-on-the-cob for breakfast. The mist continued to roll over the island, one moment clearing and revealing the rocky cliffs, the next covering it entirely. It seemed a shame to leave, but Gav had to get back for work. We were packing up our tent for the journey to Seoul, when the lifeguards told us the ferries wouldn't be running because of the fog.

In any other circumstances, we'd have happily been marooned here, but Gav had to be on stage in the evening. You can't hide the absence of a drummer, unless you have an electronic replacement. The others in the band already thought Gav was doing something wrong by exploring the country on his days off. What if he got stranded somewhere? We'd laughed and thought they were being ridiculous. This was a disaster.

Seeing our panic, a kind man offered us a lift to a village where he thought a different ferry would be more likely to leave from. We packed into his car and were thrilled to see the ferry standing by the dock. Thanking the man profusely, we rushed to the ship – and stood on deck for hours as the crew waited for the fog to clear. Many nervous hours later, we made it back to Seoul just in time for Gav's Monday night show.

Gav once again needed new drumsticks, so that week we went back to Nagwon where he tested some out. Who knew there were so many different kinds? The cost was higher than in Canada, so Gav didn't like to buy too many at a time. Finally, when I was yawning and slouching like a bored teenager – I tried to make up for the difference in our ages by being more immature – we decided to spend some time around Chongno Samga, in the centre of the city, checking out the antique shops around Insadong and then Tapkol Park.

Tapkol Park was full of hundreds of old men. Some in straw fedoras were reading newspapers on benches, some sat on newspapers in the shade of the trees. Others played a kind of chess called *paduk*, snapping down black and white counters with a vigorous flourish. One crowd was gathered around a man demonstrating calligraphy, using his wide brush to paint Chinese characters on long sheets of white paper. There was a tent set up in one corner offering other old men acupuncture sessions. Groups of men sat on the steps of the pavilion in the middle of the park, arguing the question of the day.

The park boasted several national treasures including a beautiful fifteenth-century stone pagoda, *tapkol*, its ten layers engraved with scenes of Buddha and ferocious animals. The glass that protected it was so discoloured by the smog, slats were made in it for looking through. There was also a giant stone turtle; turtles are a symbol of old age. But the most prominent and moving piece by far was a monument to Independence and to the Sam-il Movement, thirty-three heroes who rebelled against the Japanese occupation in 1919. During the occupation, crops – and even farmers – were sent to Japan to keep its armies fed. Korean children were taught to speak, think and feel Japanese. Many of these old men relaxing in the park had lived through that occupation. The murals depicted defenceless women and children being shot by expressionless, efficient Japanese soldiers.

The Koreans had resisted so vehemently that the Japanese built a prison in Seoul, ironically right beside the Independence Gate, which was erected at the end of the 1800s to show Korea's independence as a nation from the old mother state of China. The prison was built to torture and execute insurgents and was still standing, a grim reminder in red bricks. Guerrilla groups had abounded as Japan tried to suppress Korean culture. A group of teachers worked together to preserve the Korean language, which had been banned, and others published *hangul* newspapers, calling for freedom. Many writers were arrested as 'thought criminals' and died in prison.

Inscribed in stone in Tapkol Park were the words of the Declaration of Independence, drawn up on 1 March, *sam-*

il in Korean, 1919. The declaration seemed to make great efforts not to be antagonistic but to look to the future:

> We have no desire to accuse Japan of breaking many solemn treaties since 1836, nor to single out specially the teachers in the schools or government officials who treat the heritage of our ancestors as a colony of their own, and our people and their civilisation as a nation of savages, finding delight only in beating us down and bringing us under their heel.
>
> We have no wish to find special fault with Japan's lack of fairness or her contempt of our civilisation and the principles on which her state rests... neither need we, who require so urgently to build for the future, spend useless hours over what is past and gone. Our urgent need today is the settling up of this house of ours and not a discussion of who has broken it down, or what has caused its ruin...
>
> Our part is to influence the Japanese government, dominated as it is by the old idea of brute force which thinks to run counter to common and universal law, so that it will change, act honestly and in accord with the principles of right and truth...

As reserved as the declaration was, the Sam-il Movement was quashed, and as punishment the military killed and wounded thousands.

In 1995, fifty years after Korea was freed from Japanese occupation, celebrations were held as trade and peaceful relations were resumed between South Korea and Japan. The history of trade between the two countries meant a rapprochement was inevitable at some point. Now, South Korea and Japan were preparing to host the World Cup together – a clock at the top of the city hall proudly counted down the days. The men in Tapkol Park had seen much.

That night, we heard explosions, and immediately thought of North Korea and bombs, before realising it was the fourth of July, and the sound was fireworks at the US army base.

CHAPTER ELEVEN:

THE MONK AND I

Seonunsa, a head temple of the Jogye Order of Korean Buddhism, was first built during the Paekche Dynasty. Once there were 3,000 monks practising asceticism there, 189 dormitories, 89 hermitages, 144 caves. The great hall was destroyed by fire during the Japanese invasion in 1597 and reconstructed over the next couple of decades. Seonunsa is the name of the temple (-sa meaning temple) and Seonunsan the name of the mountainous area around it (-san meaning mountain).

Mountains have spiritual significance in Korea. In the country's indigenous religion, which continues to be 'an active cultural force' (Lonely Planet), mountains are where shamans commune with spirits. In the countryside, the only clearings you see on hills are for ancestral burial mounds. Koreans believe that a well-chosen burial site brings prosperity to the family of the deceased. The burial mounds themselves look like miniature hills, in a tradition that stretches back to the Paekche and Shilla kingdoms of 1,500 years ago. Mountains are not cleared for building; however industrialised a valley may be, the forest-covered mountain retains its purity. Monasteries are often situated in mountains; they were forced out of the cities long ago, and although welcome there again, perhaps they chose to stay because nature is important to Buddhists, and peacefulness is good for meditation.

After a few days in Seoul, I was ready to get back to my real Korean adventure. I'd had enough of late-night clubbing, day-trip sightseeing and rushing back for the evening show. Seoul had a cultural heritage to explore, well documented in guidebooks, but I wanted to wander again and see where I ended up. Seoul was beginning to feel superficial again; I wanted to engage with people. I wanted to be surprised. There was an old Buddhist temple called Seonunsa in a mountainous provincial park close to the sea, down the west coast again but farther south, and I hoped there'd be a bus going there when I got to the station that afternoon. If not, fate would send me somewhere else.

Standing around wearing a backpack in the express bus station seemed to be one of the best ways to meet people in Seoul. Men of all ages would come up and ask, 'Can I help you?' They could be quite bossy, though. One man asked where I was going, grabbed my ticket and marched me all the way to the gate and insisted on sitting me down in the correct waiting area, even though it was forty minutes until the bus left. They liked things to be orderly.

To escape more such assistance, I went for food. Korean bus stations, I was finding, are great places to eat. Two ladies were rolling *kimbap* at one of the food counters, and I ordered a serving, which came with a bowl of hot broth. I had also found service stations to have good snacks, and on the way to Kochang when we stopped for a break I bought hot pancakes fresh from the griddle, filled with honey, nuts and cinnamon. I ate four of them, standing in the warm evening air, surrounded by hills, pleased to be on the road again and already receiving curious smiles.

I arrived in Kochang in the dark. At 9 p.m. the station offices were closed. I spotted the bus timetable on the wall and tried deciphering the place names from the Korean script to plan my onward journey the next day. As I stood there, a Buddhist monk with pale grey robes and a perfectly smooth head, who'd been on the same bus as me, came up and asked where I was going. I felt rather hopeful of a repeat of my Sudoksa adventures, so I told him that I was heading for Seonunsa, wondering if he lived there. When he asked me if I wanted to stay at his temple for the night, I readily accepted.

He offered me the back seat of his car, which I found a little awkward, but who knew what rules different monks had to adhere to when it came to associating with unkempt foreign women? He was in his fifties with a rather serious demeanour. We pulled into a petrol station and sat in silence as the attendant filled the tank. Then the monk leaned back and handed me something. What was it? I read the packet:

'Morning Tissues.' Perhaps it was a freebie gift from the station attendant. He smiled, and I laughed. It broke the ice.

He said he would drive me to Seonunsan in the morning, so he obviously didn't live there after all. I asked the name of his temple, and he told me Yeonhwasa. We were heading into countryside. In the dark, I made out fields either side of the road. After about twenty minutes, we left the main road and arrived at a farm. He disappeared for a moment, then came out to ask if I would like to have coffee with his 'temple family'. I hesitated, stupidly saying I didn't want coffee, not knowing what would be polite, but he encouraged me to come in and we walked across a yard past tractors, dogs and a chicken coop.

In a room sparsely decorated with a huge TV, a few family photos high up above a doorway, several clocks and a roll of toilet paper hanging on the wall, presumably for cleaning hands, I met the temple family. We all sat cross-legged on the floor. They were small people, with the dark tanned complexion that comes from working outdoors, and black wavy hair cut short. I'd seen people who looked like this in the fields, squatting to pick crops as I whizzed by in a bus. Suddenly I realised how small the monk was, too, sitting on the floor and urging me to eat slices of the yellow melon that had been cut for us.

One woman wore gold jewellery and lots of gold in her teeth. She looked embarrassed. Her husband, dirty from working in the fields, refused to come into the room, and sat in the covered porch instead. They asked if I was travelling alone, *honja*, and I said yes, to *ah*s of astonishment. I tried to explain that I had a boyfriend back in the city. 'Drummer,' I said, miming. 'Hyattu Hotelo.' *Ahh!* Smiles, confused looks.

The other woman stared at me with a big, friendly smile. She asked how old I was. Then she touched my wooden bead bracelet and asked, with a palms-together bow, if I was Buddhist. I shook my head but tried to explain that I was learning about Buddhism, and said 'Sudoksa', indicating the bracelet.

Back in the car, the monk and I drove uphill along a rough track towards a neon reverse swastika, the symbol for a Buddhist temple, and a string of colourful lanterns. A rabbit froze in the headlights as we parked, and in the dark I glimpsed traditional wooden buildings. The house area was a functional wood and concrete place, where mosquitoes played crazily in the light. A woman showed me to a tiny cell-like room, raised off the ground on a platform. She wiped dead insects off the floor, turned on an electric fan and left a can of insect spray. She also brought bedding – a reed mat, a quilt for a mattress, a pillow and a cotton blanket – and pointed out the latrines beyond the end of the building.

I thanked her, left my shoes outside and crouched to get through the doorway into the stiflingly hot space, closing the door at once against mosquitoes. This was a storeroom: I was surrounded by toilet rolls, extra blankets, a sewing machine and radio, odd bits of furniture. Not quite like the sumptuous accommodation of the last monastery I'd stayed at. The floor was a bug graveyard. It was still early, as the noisily ticking clock kept telling me, but I lay my sleeping bag over the thin quilt for extra padding and managed to fall asleep. Around midnight I woke, needing desperately to pee. There was no light, so I fumbled in my backpack for my torch, but the more vain the search seemed, the more urgent my need became, so I grabbed my Morning Tissues and stumbled outside.

Fearing the bark of a guard dog, I tiptoed to the end of the house in the dark, brushing away cobwebs and mosquitoes and feeling for a light switch. The latrines were vile-smelling in the humid heat, though at least the holes in the concrete floor were covered when not in use. I was loath to uncover one, and there was no sign of a light switch. Eventually I chose the grass instead, swatting away insects and praying that my monk – or any monk – wouldn't come by at that moment.

Back in my room, sleep eluded me. My body was now accustomed to staying up until all hours in the city, and I hadn't done much to tire myself out – just eat and sit on a bus. The noisy fan only made the hot, humid air turbulent, so I turned it off, and disabled the clock by removing the battery. Peaceful, Buddhist thoughts were hard to summon. Cattle lowed in a nearby field. Outside my door, I thought I heard the occasional tock of a wooden drum. I heard one o'clock strike, then two, and three.

Clearly something was drawing me to these Buddhist temples, I reflected. I didn't for a minute intend to take up religion, but was brushing up close to an inspiring way of life, and wanted to know more.

I must have fallen asleep eventually, because I woke up to a beautiful male voice chanting outside. I lay spellbound for a while. When I looked at the time, it was 4.50 a.m. Just then, someone struck the enormous iron bell in the wooden pavilion a few metres away. Its deep sound grew loud and intense, and I felt it vibrate through me before its perfect note receded; then it struck again. I pulled on my clothes and quietly opened my door to half-daylight, and knelt on the wooden balcony. One of the women from last night was kneeling and swinging a huge wooden clanger against the bell. Finally she got up and went back towards the house, where she took wood from the massive stack of logs, and lit a fire under an iron stove.

I walked through mist and the smell of woodsmoke; it was still not fully light, and the singing was lovely. Below were fields. Above, pine forest. A little way up the hill, in the temple, the monk was alone, singing. A golden statue of Buddha looked out across the valley, lit candles glinting off the gilt, and the ceiling was covered in lotus-lanterns from which hung paper prayers. Looking for the cattle I'd heard during the night, I walked down the hill perplexed until I reached a large pond, where the noise grew loud. Frogs! I couldn't see them, but they must be there in the reeds. The pond was alive with dragonflies and birds.

The lovely quiet of the morning was suddenly rent asunder by an incredibly loud lawnmower. A man who looked as shaken by the noise as I felt – the man, I think, who'd insisted on sitting in the porch the night before – proceeded to give a brutal haircut to the lawn below the house, where the colourful paper lanterns hung. I went and spied on the monk, who had finished his singing and was looking out across the valley. It seemed inappropriate to disturb him, but he bellowed out a jolly 'Good morning!' He came down the hill and talked to the lawnmower man about the vegetables in the garden. It occurred to me that this was the extent of the temple: one monk and his temple family, growing their own food and making a living from the farm. The earth was a rich reddish brown, like the bark of the pine trees.

The air was cooler and fresher than the night before – perhaps it had rained while I slept – and swallow-like birds swooped and circled in the grayish-white sky. I visited the temple buildings while the monk sat and wrote in his room and Buddhist chants played through a speaker strung up in the trees. In the main temple, incense hung in the air. The ceiling beams, twisted and curved like the trees outside from which they had clearly been made, were painted bright yellow and pink, and a pink satin canopy hung over the small bell. Further back towards the forest was another meditation place: before the altar was a little table with a wooden bell, a brass bell, an open book, a clock and a small bronze gong. The walls were decorated with paintings, the ceiling with pink silk lotus flowers. On the step outside, long brown vegetables like thin snakes had been spread out to dry.

There was nothing ostentatious about these buildings, though they were lovingly decorated and cared for. Korean Buddhism teaches that we are all part of nature, and its buildings try to blend into their natural surroundings. They were quite different to the huge and imperialistic Buddhist temples I would later see in Japan, or those in China or Thailand with their gold roofs. Respect for nature, and oneness with it, is intrinsic to Korean Buddhism. Harmony with nature and simple, restrained elegance are Korean ideals.

Finally we were called for breakfast. A feast was laid out on a low table in the house: steaming bowls of rice mixed with violet beans, and several bowls of accompanying dishes, like hot green chilli peppers sauteed with sesame seeds, buttery potatoes and garlicky spinach-like greens, all fresh and delicious. There was ice-cold tea, which the others poured into their rice bowls at the end of the meal to get the rest of the rice, and drank like soup. Nothing wasted.

The monk, who wrote out his name for me as Seok Do Myung, had also written out directions for the next stage of my journey in English and *hangul*, so I shouldn't have any difficulty finding my way. I enquired when his temple was founded, and he said sixty years ago, explaining also that Yeonhwasa meant Pink Lotus Temple, and that the farm produced ginseng. It was now clear that his English was in fact very good, and his reticence last night was perhaps due to shyness or etiquette. We talked a little about Canada, and he produced a card of a friend of his, who worked for a golfing organisation in Vancouver. He told me of his plans to go to Los Angeles next year, home to 700,000 Koreans, and build a temple.

What an extraordinary place my wandering had brought me to. I didn't want to leave, but suddenly we were on our way.

'The bus to Seonunsa is leaving at seven o'clock, and takes forty minutes!' I was confused at first, then realised he was joking and meant his car. I shoved everything back into my backpack and got myself ready. Just down the road we picked up a teenaged boy and girl on their way to middle- and high-school. Dark-skinned with long, slender limbs and extraordinarily fine features, the girl sat up straight in the back with me, afraid even to glance in my direction, while her brother received what sounded like a good- natured lecture from the monk in the front. They got out in a village and we continued past terraced paddy fields and lush hills. Finally the sea appeared to our left, pale and shallow: Sung Hae, the West Sea, otherwise known as the Yellow Sea because of the silt that empties into it from one of China's great rivers, so that it's never blue and clear.

At the entrance to Seonunsa, my monk waved himself through the gate and we came to a stop right outside the main temple compound. He pointed out the path up the mountain, which he said was very beautiful. As we shook hands, he wished me 'happy memories of Korea'. Then he was off, returning my wave as he drove away.

Wooden painted statues of wrathful spirits towered over me as I walked through the gateway into the large courtyard. There was nobody about, though I could hear some workmen behind a tarpaulin where restoration work was being done. A man emerged with a spray gun and a canister on his back, and did some spraying here and there, presumably against flies and mosquitoes. I'd seen it being done all over the area, white smoke billowing out of farm buildings and restaurants. I caught sight of a monk but he disappeared into a dormitory hall.

Removing my shoes, I walked across the polished but worn wooden floor of the great hall. The ceiling beams had once been ornately painted; I could still make out the dragons on the upper beams, faded with age but all the more beautiful for it. I bowed to the Buddha as I now knew how, putting my palms together and lowering my head, then dropping to my knees, touching first my forehead to the ground, and finally my forearms with palms upturned. The role of the Buddha statue is to remind you of your fundamental nature, to help you discover it. In a way, the Buddha is your own image, and you are bowing to your own self; not worshipping another being but acknowledging your foundation, through which you are connected to everything in the universe. I stayed there a little while, contemplating the peaceful moment, before going back out to the still-empty courtyard.

It was only 8 a.m. It felt good to be out so early. The good breakfast, green chillies included, had set me up for the day. The sky was clearing to blue and the temperature rising as I started up the path through the woods beside a rocky stream, fanning my face with my hat to keep buzzing flies at bay. Passing a six-hundred-year-old pine tree and a deep, cool cave used as a shrine, I soon found the trail up the mountain towards the other hermitages of the temple.

It was a strain hiking up the steep trail in the heat with my heavy backpack, which contained a tent and sleeping bag in case I needed them. I was ready for a rest when I came to a hermitage called Dosolam. Two Chindo dogs stood at the entrance, their thick hair a gorgeous creamy white, with dark eyes and pointed ears, somewhat like huskies. I knew about Chindo dogs because I'd read in the *Korea Herald* that President Kim Dae-jung had presented a couple of them to Chairman Kim Jong-il during the summit talks. They come from an island in the south-west of the peninsula and are known as loyal watchdogs. These ones quietly watched me pass.

I found myself in a stunning courtyard: pale sand, a shady tree, a wooden temple looking out across the valley to forest-covered craggy mountains. Conscious of looking sweaty and red-faced, I bowed to two monks sitting in the shade of their dormitory's balcony. One was an older, corpulent man with glasses and a beatific smile. His younger companion made the fluttering downward hand gesture which looks like 'put it down' or 'stay there', but actually means 'come here'. Sheepish but grateful I crossed the courtyard and sat with them in the shade, where a woman brought me a glass of orange juice.

The young monk's round, smiling face made him look much younger than the thirty-five years he claimed. He wore a pristine white T-shirt and beige, loose-weave cotton trousers held up by a brown leather belt: monk chic. After asking about my travels, he presented me with a satin pouch with a Buddhist book inside, and attached it to my backpack. Monks had been feeding me, driving me around and paying for my bus fares, I thought, and now they were giving me gifts again.

'Thank you so much!' I said. 'That's so kind of you.'

Rolling his eyes and laughing as if he'd heard it many times, he said, 'Oh, Korean monks are *so kind!*' Then, as a loud clanging of gongs began in the temple, he led me up steep steps to another small temple built upon rock, where people were meditating before golden bodhisattvas. A young nun stood back from the building out on the rock, staring towards the temple, motionless except for her singing lips: she never seemed to pause for breath, her voice never faltered, and I felt it almost an intrusion to watch. But I couldn't keep my eyes from this mesmerising sight.

On the way down, the monk stopped to show me a relief carving of a seated Buddha in a pink cliff. It must have been at least ten metres high. He said it was built by Chinese artists sometime in the sixth century.

'May I ask, which part of Canada are you from? I have visited Vancouver,' he said.

'Really? I've been living in Toronto, the other side of the country, very far away. But what were you doing in Vancouver?' I asked, imagining some sort of Buddhist monk convention.

He had a mischievous look on his face. 'Bungee jump!'

They seemed to enjoy life, these monks, so I was taken by surprise when, as I held out my hand to shake his in thanks, he simply pressed his hands together and bowed, explaining: 'Boy and girl never hand must touch.'

I retrieved my backpack, and the monk pointed me in the right direction and said goodbye.

Their lives seemed a curious mix of life-loving fun and strict piety. Musing how it was decided what monks could and couldn't do, I followed the path uphill past the Youngmoon Caves, strewn with picnickers' rubbish, then past craggy rocks to Unicorn Peak. From there I saw again the Buddha carved into the pink rock face, now starkly visible for miles around, surrounded by nothing but green. A little higher was a smooth rock face where the monks and nuns, having finished their meditation, were sitting and talking. Otherwise, all was quiet. The summer rain and sunshine kept the forested hills sparkling deep green. Brilliant leafy valleys stretched out before me, and I had only the dragonflies for company.

Which way was the sea? I'd lost my bearings, so I followed the ridge past a sign to something called Chamdangam, the spiders' webs hanging across the path a sure sign I was the only walker up here today. Wearing my floppy hat against the sun, I got into the habit of flapping my bandanna in front of my face as I walked to break the webs, like a member of the religious sect who sweep the ground before them to avoid killing an ant. I was feeling eccentric and in a magical place where anything could happen.

Rambling feet and rambling thoughts go well together. The energy and rhythm of walking alone encourages thoughts to develop, helps us sometimes to remember what is important. Early Christians in England knew this: the poem 'The Wanderer' is about seeking both physically and spiritually. These Buddhist monks valued the simple, quiet, isolated life, and so, for the moment, did I.

Lush green hills gave way to vegetable gardens then to a circle of natural wooden buildings surrounding a spotless empty courtyard, where a rough stone trough stood, filled with spring water. I took the scoop and poured some cool water over my face. The empty courtyard of Chamdangam, another hermitage of Seonunsa, basked in sunlight, absolutely still in the heat of the day. Suddenly, a car drove up, breaking the silence. A few monks got out and went to sit on a rock in the shade of a tree. When I put my palms together to bow to them, they waved me over.

'Hello! I am Chi-bong.' The young man who spoke English was another cool monk. Slim, with very short hair, he wore a wide-brimmed straw hat, his pale grey cotton T-shirt and monk-pants loose on his slender frame. Oh – and he had a lovely smile and sparkling eyes. There were just six monks living here, he said. He had arrived five months ago, from a hermitage on Cheju Island, the semitropical volcanic island far south of the mainland. He was allowed to stay at any temple he liked, but he'd chosen this place here because it was so beautiful and peaceful. Just as he said that, the sky was filled with the noise of jets flying low overhead. We laughed together.

I'd heard these jets before, and assumed they were military. Yes, he said, there was a base nearby and they trained a few days a week – but other than that it was quiet here. For me, the moment was a rare reminder that this peaceful Buddhist country, with its huge American military and air force bases, was always on alert against attack from the North.

A woman who seemed to be one of the 'temple family' who looked after the place had been staring at me entranced. Now she asked if I had eaten. Not since breakfast seven hours ago, and I was starving. She led me through the kitchen, past a table covered with mushrooms drying in the sun, to a room with a television and an open door looking out over the fields. Here she sat me down in front of a low table and switched on a fan, went back into the kitchen and reappeared five minutes later with a large tray of different vegetable dishes. She packed a bowl with rice from the steamer, and sat down to watch me eat. I nodded and smiled at her as I ate, embarrassed but thankful, trying to express how good it all was. All the food was grown here, and it tasted delicious. Buddhist monks learned to live off the land when they were driven into the mountains, and clearly they had developed it into a fine art.

I went back outside to sit on the rock and chat with Chibong. He asked about my reasons for coming to Korea, what it was like travelling alone here. He had travelled with a backpack and tent himself in Europe with a friend, visiting Germany, Spain, France, Switzerland, Italy: he loved climbing mountains and ice, and had made it to the top of Mont Blanc. I wondered how a monk could afford to travel around Europe, but wasn't sure how to ask. In the Koryo Dynasty, Buddist monks got rich from commerce, farming, wine making and even loaning money at high interest. In those days, Buddhism was a state religion, merging philosophy with political power. How did monks survive these days?

'I know this is a personal question,' I ventured, 'but what work do you do here?'

He looked surprised, as he stated the obvious: 'Meditate.'

He asked about my boyfriend's job.

'He's a musician. A drummer,' I said. 'He plays at a big hotel in Seoul.'

'Classical?'

I shook my head. 'Rock.'

He smiled, and asked which hotel the band played at. I told him, and he said he'd visited the Hyatt one time with his friend and had a coffee. It was hard to imagine Chi-bong sitting in his grey monk clothes surrounded by designer boutiques and quarrelling funk musicians. Just then, three more young monks came by, looking like any other skinny lads in their early twenties, with baggy trousers and T-shirts and hats, and towels around their necks.

'Today it's too hot to meditate, so they are going swimming,' explained Chi-bong.

The women brought watermelon, which I happily munched. As I prepared to be off so that Chi-bong could join his friends at the river, he said I could stay there for a night if I liked. It was tempting. I was getting along well with Chi-bong, enjoying his smile. But I didn't want to take too much and abuse the monks' kindness. While I'd have been thankful of a bed for the night if I'd really needed it, it was still only early afternoon and I had plenty of time to find a place to stay. So I gave Chi-bong my phone number, and told him to call if he came mountain climbing in my country. He seemed happy.

'But will you remember me?' he asked, smiling shyly.

Are you flirting with me, I thought, and brushed away the notion. I laughed, thinking of how many calls I get from Korean monks, and assured him I would.

Buddhist monks seemed to be guiding my journey as they welcomed me to their homes in these isolated places. Was it a lonely life here? I know how much I need company and love, but sometimes you need to remove yourself from the company of people who know you, in order to think about who you are and what you want out of life. Han Bi-ya, Korean author of *Daughter of the Wind: Three and a Half Times Around the Earth on Foot*, says she travels not 'by herself' but 'with herself' – that by travelling solo she has nurtured a dialogue with herself and learned more about herself and how to cope with difficulty.

The monks appeared happy. As I would read later, an important element of Korean Buddhism is that you can't cling to happiness or sadness; you walk peacefully and freely towards enlightenment. Everything that happens teaches you something and you move forward, whatever is happening. The only way to be satisfied in life is to learn your true nature.

Chi-bong's responsibility as a monk was to meditate. Meditation, according to Seon (better known to us as Zen) Master Daehaeng in her book *Wake Up and Laugh*, is not just about sitting. 'Spiritual practice is done through your mind, not through your body.' In this busy age, she says, living itself – eating, working, driving, loving, sleeping – should all become practising Seon. Even bungee jumping, climbing Mont Blanc. She speaks of *gwan*: mindfulness, observing, being aware. And of letting go things that are unimportant. We must search within ourselves to live with joy and freedom.

Hiking back down towards the park's entrance, I found a shop where I bought a bandanna with a map of the park on it. What a clever idea. There was also a sign with information about the places I'd been. When I started copying some details into my notebook, the shopkeeper came out and gave me his last tattered copy of an English-language booklet. He seemed proud that I would spend all day hiking in his national park.

Eventually, it was time to leave Seonunsan and find a nice place to stay the night. Pyonsan, according to my guidebook, had a beach, Pyonsanbando. I decided to try to get there.

CHAPTER TWELVE:

OUT WITH THE BOYS IN PYONSAN

The Korean peninsula at its very north has a long border with China; Korea looks like a spur off China's north-east coast. Archaeological evidence shows Chinese pottery spread from China to Korea as early as two millennia BC. During the Three Kingdoms period, the Koguryo Kingdom started to extend into Manchuria (China) at around the time the Paekche Kingdom was forging links with Japan. The Sui Dynasty of China saw Koguryo as a threat, and sent huge armies in, but the Koreans were well-trained fighters and the result was a truce. The succeeding Tang Dynasty of China teamed up with the Shilla Kingdom to defeat the rival Koguryo finally in 668. Shilla developed a close association with

Tang China, and imported Chinese medicine, astronomy, music, literature, administration and laws.

Buddhism was imported from China, and so was Confucianism. Confucius lived in China from 551 to 479 BC, but Korea is said to be the most Confucian nation in Asia. Although we tend to think of Confucius simply as a wise man (Confucius he say…), Confucianism is a strict and complex system of ethics that reveres education, respect for elders, deference to authority, male superiority, etc. Rules govern every type of social relationship, subjecting them to a hierarchical structure. The information you learn when introduced to someone determines how you behave towards one another.

I referred to the monk's handwritten directions and caught a bus to Kochang, then from Kochang to Puan, and from Puan to Pyonsan. I was falling asleep on the bus in the still-hot late afternoon as I saw what looked like Pyonsanbando fly past the window.

Jumping out at the next stop, I asked a group of teenage lads the way, and they pointed me back in the right direction. As I was making my way along the road, one breathless skinny boy caught up with me and said he wanted to help me. I declined his gallant offer to carry my pack, but happily agreed to have some English-speaking company on my walk. We continued along making pleasant conversation. His name was Oh Jung-seok, and in fact he wasn't a teenager at all but a twenty-two-year-old student of Hotel Management at Cheju University. He had an endearing way of apologising abjectly for his English, which was actually pretty good. I was the first foreigner he'd ever seen in Pyonsan, he said. I felt honoured.

At Pyonsanbando, Jung-seok found me a cheap room in a guesthouse right on the beach, with a window looking out to sea, the curtain billowing in the breeze. Perfect. Leaving my bag, I went back out for a cold drink, offering to buy Jung-seok one for his kindness. Nice as it was to be meeting people, I was really tired, badly needed a shower, and didn't have the energy to chat. He said he'd be pleased to show me into Inner Pyonsan next day, and waved a smiling goodbye. I took my beer down to the beach, where the sun was setting, turning orange, then pink as it sank; there were islands silhouetted grey. I hadn't heard waves for some time, not since Tokjokdo.

Back at the deserted *minbak* (guesthouse), I found the shower at the end of the corridor. The facilites were small and basic but clean: concrete floors, cold water and buckets. I opened the door of my room and stepped up barefoot onto the raised floor. There was a fan, quilts laid out on the linoleum for bedding, a pillow. The cell-like simplicity and the sound of the sea outside my window were calming.

Down the road were a few quiet restaurants. A friendly wave beckoned me into a place that looked expensive. But the people spoke English and understood when I told them I had little money. They cooked me a fantastic meal of steaming, spicy instant noodles with egg and green onion, and side-bowls of rice, kimchi, tofu and potatoes, and charged the tiny amount of 2,000 won when I left. In fact I didn't have change so they asked me to drop in next day to pay, and waved goodbye, calling 'See you again!'

I strolled down the beach, the sand soft underfoot. Campers were sitting around fires. Others were walking or sitting together, sharing a drink. A woman sat on a wooden bed, massaging her feet. The beach was beautiful, a bright moon shining on the waves and the stretches of flat wet sand where the tide had gone out. Out at sea were the lights of fishing boats, and above were stars. I went home and fell asleep to the sound of the waves, waking to the same sound about ten hours later. The best night's sleep in memory.

Mist covered the mountains but the sun was heating a hazy sky. I went for a swim, then walked along the sand. Two ladies wearing cotton gloves and headscarves were clearing litter into bags. At the end of the beach there was a campground, but only a few tents – the season didn't officially start until next day, 8 July.

Busloads of children of four or five started pouring onto the sand, kept in line by teachers with megaphones. Each group had its own bright uniform, including matching hat and daypack, in yellow or blue. One group, discovering crabs for the first time, was shrieking and running about wildly, limbs flailing. A teacher showed the children that crabs were harmless, calming them for a few minutes. The moment she stepped away one of the kids set them all off shrieking again. Their giddy excitement was infectious.

The mist was gradually clearing and the mountains were calling me. I set off walking. The coast road was hair-raising, with speeding buses and an inordinate number of concrete mixers en route to some big construction project, and I was glad to turn off it. By contrast, the road which wound inland and gradually uphill was silent and passed through dark green hills and beautiful farmland, fields of tobacco and onions spreading away to the hills, and tiny farm buildings at the roadside with garlic hanging to dry under the eaves. I stopped to cool off in the shade of every tree I passed.

When I reached the entrance to Inner Pyonsan National Park, the heat was intense and I truly began to question my sanity for being out in the midday sun. A warden was lying under a thatched shelter taking a siesta, but he woke when I arrived and, although surprised, gave me a helpful map in return for the 1,000-won entrance fee. The closest peak, it seemed, was Ssangsonbong, just over a kilometre away, so I thought I'd give that a try.

It didn't take me long to figure out that this kilometre was an almost vertical one. But it was peaceful alone with the crickets in the forest. Eventually I came to a rock on the edge of the mountain, with a breeze and a breathtaking view of glistening forest sweeping from the ridge, 400 metres above sea level, all the way down to the valley where the farms began. The breeze smelled of heat and pine. The wind blowing through the trees sounded like the sea.

I spent the whole afternoon wandering the pathways. At one point, I emerged from the trees to the jutting edge of the mountain where a helpful sign read 'Danger – Falling!'

Standing amidst massive boulders on the cliff edge, I could see all the way across to a sea inlet where an island seemed to hover in the mist. There was a small blue-green lake at the foot of this mountain. I scrambled down a steep, shingly path for an hour, and finally found myself overlooking waterfalls. My legs ached, my arms and shoulders were smarting with sunburn. I stood knee-deep in a pool surrounded by crystal-shaped rocks covered with moss, and poured cool water over my head.

When I finally reached the farther exit of the park and bought a cold drink from its shop, the last bus was leaving, but going in the wrong direction, so I started out on foot for the road back to Pyonsanbando, not much relishing the idea. I'd come much further inland from where I'd started out. I was weak, having eaten nothing all day except two small yellow melons for breakfast on the beach. It was silly to have left so much to chance, to plan so poorly.

I'd got as far as the main road when I saw a farm where a large group of people were sitting on newspapers around a barbecue. They waved me over to join them. After confirming that I was travelling *honja* and indicating that I had been hiking in Nae (Inner) Pyonsan all day, I was promptly treated to slices of barbecued eel fresh off the grill, slathered in hot red sauce with sesame seeds, wrapped in a lettuce leaf, and washed down with a shot glass of clear 'Korean whisky', or soju. Sure, I was hungry, but it all tasted amazingly good. I would have loved to stay, but dusk was already beginning to fall – and I had far to go.

I hadn't walked on for more than ten minutes when a truck stopped. The driver said he'd seen me earlier at the entrance to the park, so he knew how exhausted and in need of a lift I must be. Pyonsan turned out to be much further off than I'd thought. He dropped me off at the town and I had only a kilometre's walk to the beach as dusk was falling. The people of Pyonsan were taking care of this errant foreigner, all because I'd taken the trouble to travel around their country.

On the sand, I stood in the waves, letting the cool saltwater soothe my aching feet. In the grey half-light, the sky almost melted into the sea. Between the dark, rocky promontories on either side of the bay, waves rolled in to shore, caught in the moonlight, casting shadows before they broke. I stayed transfixed, thinking of chance meetings and magical moments, until I was shivering.

The people at the restaurant had another friendly welcome for their least profitable customer, cooking me up a revitalising bowl of *ramyun* noodles with mushroom salad and other vegetable side dishes for a minuscule sum. As I left, feeling infinitely better, one inebriated man called out, 'Do you want friend? I favour you!' The woman who ran the restaurant laughed and waved him away, shouting, 'Good night!'

Making my way back to the room I was accosted by a large, chubby young man who promptly told me he was thirty-five and known as Mr Che. A funny and rather charismatic character, he checked to see my accommodation arrangements were satisfactory, then commanded me to join him and his friends. 'Drinking!' he demanded.

Well, why ever not. It would be rude to say no.

So I sat at the table on the beach with Mr Che's brother and friends, learning the etiquette of drinking OB Light. Mr

Che instructed me how to tilt my glass Korean-style when he poured beer. To pour, you must hold the bottle with your right hand and touch or cup your wrist or forearm with the left. You do something similar when offering or receiving money. And when someone offers you an empty glass, you hold it while they pour for you. He taught me how to shout 'Kombae!' for cheers, and encouraged me to taste the chewy dried squid, ochinga, they were handing round as a beer snack. He asked how old my boyfriend was. 'Twenty-two,' I replied. He pointed to a scrawny kid who looked about twelve, and exclaimed, 'Mr Kim also is twenty-two!' It was hard to explain the difference without offending.

After I'd sat for a while chatting with the boys from Pyonsan, they decided to drive to Kyokpo, a village down the coast road. What is it about small-town boys that they always want to drive somewhere? I preferred to sit on the beach, but they said it was only eight kilometres and that Mr Kim had stopped drinking OB Light after one glass so that he could drive. It seemed churlish to refuse, and we set off for Kyokpo, Mr Kim trying to demonstrate the television in his car and navigate the road at the same time.

It was a boring drive to a seaside resort town of amusement arcades, shooting galleries and rides, all still closed because the season didn't start until the next day. There was nothing to do but stand around while the large Mr Che fed coins into a machine. He didn't win the cuddly toy. We drove back in a subdued mood. I excused myself from going on to the coffee shop and had to insist rather forcefully this time on going home.

It appeared I had been altogether wrong about Koreans being unfriendly. The problem is partly that the happy, warm side of the Korean nature, the Buddhist side if you will, is countered by the solemn, serious Confucian side, which imposes strict rules of etiquette. Status can be determined by age, job, schooling, wealth, and that imposes rules on how to behave with those around you. It was now clear why people always asked my age. And it explained why Sean Kim said Koreans aren't sure how to handle foreigners. Not that etiquette is always a bad thing – some might say we could benefit from a little more of it in the West. I escaped most of the requirements of etiquette, however, simply by being a traveller. I was a guest, female, travelling alone without much money. If I showed suitable respect, it seemed I would be looked after.

A refreshing morning swim was first thing on the agenda the next day, followed by a walk down the sand, watching the crabs bury themselves in holes. I'd slept soundly again, and my muscles felt stretched in the best possible way. Mr Che emerged from his house when I was preparing to leave. He made sure I stood at the right bus stop, buying me an iced lolly for the ride and giving me a goodbye bear-hug. While I waited for the bus, I watched a woman cutting turnips and cabbages into huge bowls for making kimchi. I wished I didn't have to go back to Seoul; I wished Gav could come here instead.

The bus drove through lush valleys that fell away into picturesque mudflats, where old people squatted on their haunches to poke around for shellfish. It was a country bus, and everyone seemed to be carrying large bundles into town. A thin, frail-looking old man, who'd smiled at me with rotten teeth, gallantly helped a lady lift her bundles down onto the street when we got to Puan where I was to change buses.

It was lunchtime, and groups of schoolkids shouted 'Hi!' and 'Hello!' at me, giggling wide-eyed when they got a response. A lady with an umbrella smiled and gestured that I was very tall, and gave me a thumbs-up. In the market, a man had a crowd around as he auctioned off enormous fish with flapping gills. I bought bags of plums and cucumbers, and a pretty embroidered cushion.

The Excellent Express bus sped through countryside where men fished along the riverbank, and beautiful white herons stood and stared into shallow water. In the middle of a weir, a grey heron perched, looking for fish. Low farmhouses with traditional curly roofs painted orange or blue stood alone against the green paddy fields, so much more beautiful than the occasional modern glass and stone building.

The fact that I was fast on my way back to Seoul hit home when I heard a young woman behind me cleaning her teeth, then saw her staring into her mirror for ages. In the country I never saw women so obsessed with how pretty they looked. They were usually busy working in fields or in the market, wearing loose headscarves, loose clothing, boots and gloves.

The road was heavy with traffic but we sped along in the bus lane, back to the big smoke.

CHAPTER THIRTEEN:

THE BEER THAT MADE KOREA FAMOUS

Shamanism is common to many ancient cultures (the word 'shaman' originated in Siberia). I'd been curious ever since seeing a sign on the slopes of Inwangsan in Seoul forbidding 'camping, fires and Shamanism'. In Korea, the shaman or mudang *offers a sacrifice to the spirits of rocks and trees and mountains and, through singing and dancing in a kind of trance, begs the spirits to intercede in the affairs of humans — from harvests and fishing to marriage and examinations. Frowned on by some in modern Korea, it is an ineradicable part of the cultural heritage, even designated an important 'Intangible Treasure'.*

The shaman is often a woman, who communes with the spirits through dance. This popular village practice was persecuted by the

154

Confucians of the Choson Dynasty, and with its lack of written doctrine was often frowned upon as the superstition of uneducated women. And yet it persisted, with much crossover between Buddhism and shamanism, though Buddhism is seen by many Koreans as intellectually superior.

Poor Gav: I almost didn't want to tell him about my exhilarating adventures. And he, who couldn't get away, almost didn't want to know. In the space of a few days, I'd met monks, eaten astonishing food, hiked in mountains and swum in the Yellow Sea. And he'd played 'September' and 'Mustang Sally' and 'Get Down On It' several more times. At least he'd been getting to know some other musicians, and taken his Aussie friends to Nagwon. It was awkward between us at first – I worried we might be drifting apart – but not for long. I gave him a wooden Buddhist necklace I'd bought for him, and he was very pleased with it.

It was dark all day that first day back, with the clouds low over Namsan, and now the rain was really lashing down, the wind rattling the windows. A monsoonal rainstorm, I supposed.

Just as we were falling asleep the night before, on my first night back in Seoul after those peaceful days in Cheollabuk Province, we heard a woman somewhere nearby scream, and scream again, over and over, piercing the night in a horrible way, then ranting hysterically, angrily. Back to the madness of Seoul, the pollution, the spitting, the roaring traffic. The rubbish piled on street corners awaiting pickup left a lingering putrid smell in the air – until the thunder broke and it rained hard for twelve hours, like today. June, July and August are the rainy season, and now by mid July it was so humid that even when it wasn't raining, your clothes were damp as soon as you went outside. The noise of the air conditioners never stopped. There was a strange bug that had made its home on the screen window of our bedroom. We called it the wind-up bug, because we were reading Haruki Marukami's book *The Wind-up Bird Chronicle*, and because this bug made a noise exactly like a wind-up toy with a crazed laugh. It went: zzww, zzzwwiw, ZZWWIW, ZZZZWIIWW, ZZZZZZZWWIWW – heh heh heh. Zww, zzww, zzzwwiw, ZZZWWIW, ZZZZZWWIWWW – heh heh heh.

And then there was the pleasure of being woken up on a Saturday morning from a deep sleep when the vendors drove their trucks into the neighbourhood and competed in decibels for local business. They shouted through booming bullhorns with the intensity of an air-raid warning to advertise their excellent service, ending with a list of their wares. KIM! KIMMM! Yes, the most popular surname in Korea was also the word for dried seaweed.

There was a frail old man who lived in the apartment next to ours. Every day we saw him squatting on his heels outside the front door, having a cigarette, and the rest of the time we heard his hacking cough, heard him clearing his throat, summoning phlegm from its very depths until it all erupted in one evil-sounding spit. He barely acknowledged us usually when we passed him at the doorway. But the next day, a lovely thing happened. Deep Throat, as I referred to him, asked in English,

'How are you?'

'Fine, thanks,' we replied, too surprised to know what to say.

'Have a nice day!' he said with an American drawl. 'Take it easy!'

The people in the tiny local shops were also getting friendlier. The lady at the video shop refused to let me pay extra for returning the video a day late. Now that the shop owners realised we were here for a while, they said hello when I came in to pick up groceries – grape juice and noodle packets and beer, mostly. We'd been getting sick of the taste of the Korean beers, OB and Hite and Cass, which all had a slightly soapy, gassy taste. We'd resorted to buying German Pilsner at 4,000 won a large bottle instead. But we were absolutely delighted to find a T-shirt on a stall in Itaewon that read: 'OB, the Beer that made Korea Famous.' *Where?* Another tourist magazine claimed soju 'along with whisky and vodka is worldwide famous as a high proof liquor'. Walk into any bar in the world and they'll have soju…

Alcohol was first introduced to Korea from China. Soju was often distilled in Buddhist monasteries, which was how they made some of their wealth. Other alcoholic drinks were infused with herbs believed to be medicinal. But these days Scotch whisky was also hugely popular, in spite of being terribly expensive compared to soju. In the bars like J.J. Mahoney's or the Hard Rock Cafe, there were walls full of lockers where people kept their bottle of whisky until the next visit.

In a shop in Itaewon I found a CD of Korean traditional drumming by a group called SamulNori that livened up my evenings at home. Their rhythms and music came from the folk tradition of *nongak*, from village farmers' bands and travelling troupes, and songs performed at shamanistic ceremonies, with a contemporary interpretation. Shamanistic music in Korea is both religion and entertainment. One of SamulNori's songs is a type of narrative prayer that would have been sung by shamans to promote health and prosperity or ensure spiritual support for a building project. According to an ethnomusicologist quoted on the liner notes, 'Silence gives way to a mesmeric tolling of the gong, slow thuds on a drum accelerate to shrill-pitched rapid strikes. Climaxes are built and subside peacefully in waves.' That's exactly how it sounded. When it began, it was so faint you could barely hear it, as if the band was approaching up a country lane; shouts accompanied the different rhythms that combined gradually into a loud cacophony, as I imagined the drummers reaching the village. No wonder people were impressed when I told them my boyfriend was a drummer at the Hyatt. Drumming had quite a tradition here.

Contemporary Koreans were attracted to the shamanistic notion of harmony. The shaman ritual strove for harmony between human and nature, social harmony between humans, family harmony between the living and the dead and between parents and children, and individual harmony. Harmony was a central concept in Korean life. The Korean flag centred on a Taoist yin-yang symbol of the harmony of opposites.

And here I was, trying to make some sort of harmony out of the two sides of my life in Korea, city life and the village life, westernised life and Buddhist life.

I was getting to enjoy my lone night-walks around Seoul, especially when the rain had cleared the air. Since nobody talked to me in Seoul anyway, I wore a Walkman and listened to music. From the road around Namsan, on a clear night you could see the millions of lights of the sprawling city, TV billboards, the war memorial lit up, the neon crosses of Christian churches. My last attempt to sample nightlife in Seoul had taken me to Shinchon, a university district, where dark sidestreets bristled with brilliant flashing vertical signs *Blade-runner*-style, but yielded only amusement arcades with dance machines and the usual quiet coffee shops. And then I couldn't find a taxi willing to take me home. Usually, I just went on a long, long walk, watching people, and then I went to Click to research and write.

Itaewon was still good for a night out, though, when Gav finished work or on his night off. We tended to spend time with the guys from Adelaide, who were good fun but really young, in their early twenties. Same as Gav, but he seemed older. I felt so out of place when they were all talking about music, bands I'd never heard of, guitar chords. In insecure moments I wondered if Gav would rather spend time having an easy laugh with them than struggling to get along with me. But we had a good time when we went to the hole-in-the-wall dance bar Stompers. Walking up Hooker Hill we passed US army tough-guys, bare-chested in gangs with their shirts tied around their waists and their crew cuts, sweaty and tense as they stood around clutching beer bottles outside, sick of being in Korea and itching for a fight. But inside Stompers (which, like Hollywood, was off-limits to soldiers), all was relaxed and easy-going, and many a night went by with mad dancing and drinking and laughing, and trying to avoid being given tequila shots by the owner.

One night the two of us danced together in that unreserved way a few drinks will bring on, and Gav decided to try a new move that showed off his drummer's biceps, suddenly grabbing me by the waist and scooping me up in the air! He tilted me back and I shrieked, while Gav realised I wasn't built like a little ballerina and he wasn't sure he could hang on... 'Put me down!' I pleaded, but Gav was terrified he would drop me on the concrete floor and so, to avoid that, he dropped to his knees, severely bruising them in the process. Ah, Gav. The zealous romantic, with bruised knees.

The Australians had been in Seoul longer than Gav's band and were nearing the end of their contract, preparing to return to Adelaide. So on Friday night, instead of going clubbing, we went shopping with Adam and Andy, the bass player and guitarist, at Tongdaemun Market. This was the other major market at the Great East Gate of the old city wall, open all night until five in the morning. We'd been by day and found the usual combination of everything from plumbing supplies to yellow melons, as well as more unusual wares such as fried silkworm pupae sold from a big barrel for snack food and a salesman expounding the merits of the large snake around his shoulders, surrounded by a group of mesmerised men. Koreans eat snake for its libido-enhancing qualities, along with eel, deer antlers, seal's penis, and rather less disgustingly, ginseng.

When we visited Tongdaemun after Good Vibes knocked off at 2 a.m., we found Adam and Andy already in a soju tent, eating steamed mussels with potato pancakes. I tasted the mussels and they were among the best I'd ever eaten. Adam, tall and skinny with very long hair and a wide smile, was busy charming the cook, who seemed to have adopted him. Adam was in love with all Korean women. 'They call it yellow fever, man,' he said, shaking his head, 'and I've got it.' He said it in such an affectionate way that you had to laugh, in spite of the unfortunate terminology. He kept us entertained with inside stories of working in the wine industry in Australia, such as when someone lost a whole vat of wine down the drain, and they had to pump it back out again and disinfect it, before bottling it.

We bought cans of OB and wandered around the stalls. At night most of the stalls were in wholesale warehouses eight storeys high, neon palaces filled with bargain clothes. As it was late and quiet, some owners were asleep behind their counters and we had to wake them if we wanted to find out prices or try something on. It made the bargaining a bit harder when you'd woken the poor owner up. But it was still addictive wandering about in the middle of the night and haggling. Adam managed to get prices down further by complaining with good humour that he was only a poor *hoju*, an Australian with Australian dollars, and pretended to be a kangaroo. He made people laugh. He and Andy ended up with loads of hip T-shirts and shoes, and shook their heads morosely thinking of what little entertainment

Adelaide would offer at this hour. When we emerged finally outdoors again, bags of clothes were piled up on the ground ready to be shipped off trucks, and people were sitting down to breakfast at the food stalls.

Good Vibes were to be measured for new stage costumes that would take a sizeable chunk out of the next pay cheque. There was talk of leather waistcoats and tasselled trousers.

Gav was growing increasingly disenchanted with his band. At a recent rehearsal, Leroy the lead singer kept forgetting the words to 'La Vida Loca'. In an hour of practice, he was only able to get four lines right. Meanwhile Dean was still trying to line up a gig for when this one ended, feeling rather stressed about how difficult it had been, and he thought new costumes would put them in a better position.

To make matters worse, the tailor was outside Seoul at another US army base, and so our Sunday would be spent on a 'band day out'. Everyone wanted to spend the day sitting in a bar drinking, surrounded by US soldiers. But since we'd come all this way from Itaewon, Gav and I wanted to see somewhere different. After he'd been measured by the tailor and moaned at by the others, we fled by taxi and train to nearby Suwon.

Hwasong Fortress in Suwon was built between 1794 and 1796 by King Chongno for his father's tomb. Chongno wanted to move the capital here; he set up a provincial government office and started to build a Royal Country Palace. His attempt to move the capital away from Seoul was unsuccessful, however, and the structure deteriorated for two centuries, burned down and collapsed in places, but was rebuilt in the late seventies and is now a source of great pride. In a wooden pavilion stands an astonishing bell, three and a half metres high, weighing over twelve tons, rung every hour as a symbol of the Confucian values of eternal prosperity and filial piety, which Chongno showed in caring for his father's grave.

The city was built around Hwasong Fortress, now one of Korea's Unesco Cultural Heritage sites. Grey brick walls followed the ridge of the hill, interrupted every now and then by a sentry tower with scary demon faces. A green belt surrounded the walls, and since the city life went on either side of them, every now and then we found one of the sentry towers being used for a game of chess, or as a quiet place to read the newspaper.

We walked all the way around the walls, then, back where we started at the area called Paltanmun, we discovered narrow backstreets full of small bustling restaurants and bars and buzzing patios. We found a place called Live Bar, and happily ensconced ourselves to drink reasonably priced European beer while listening to Radiohead and Oasis. The young people running the place were welcoming – one of them played a flute, another showed us her tiny kitten and let it play on our table. By the time we left in search of dinner, they had taken our photo to put on the wall.

The unpretentious restaurant we found was equally friendly. When we asked the young waiters what food was on offer, they seemed to be saying *ochinga*. I thought I knew what it meant but to check I borrowed the waiter's pen and drew a picture of a squid. No, no, he said, and took the pen and drew a little conical hat on my squid. I was puzzled, so he drew two creatures with tentacles, one with a round head and one with a triangular head, and gave them different names. Aha! Octopus had round heads, squid had triangular heads. As we were their last customers for the night, the young waiters joined us over dinner and insisted we seal our friendship with shots of soju.

This national drink, sometimes called Korean whisky, was firewater that could be picked up for a mere 2,000 won a bottle practically anywhere. It had all the refined qualities of paint stripper, and a sickly smell that's hard to forget. All the posters advertising it showed pretty, wholesome young girls caressing the green bottles in lush mountain settings, as if they washed their long, clean hair with the stuff, or as if it were good for the complexion. But it actually resulted in horrible drunkenness and excruciating hangovers. Unfortunately, it was hard to avoid sometimes. Having a shot of soju together was part of the culture.

Before we staggered out, the young waiters wrote down their contact information in my notebook, carefully including name, email, 'HP' number, age and height. They were as debilitated by the soju as we are.

Back in Seoul, I typed up a story on the fortress at Suwon for the *Korea Herald* Weekender section and submitted it along with another couple of ideas I'd been tinkering with. One night, checking my email at Click, I jumped with joy to see a message from a newspaper back home accepting my piece on the Sudoksa monastery. I wondered what the *Korea Herald* would make of my latest one.

CHAPTER FOURTEEN:

GIRLS' NIGHT OUT IN KAMPO

In the seventh century, the Shilla king enlisted the help of the Tang Dynasty in China to overcome the rival Paekche and Koguryo kingdoms. Then he drove out the Chinese, and the Shilla capital, Kyungju, became the capital of the newly unified peninsula. Artistry and Buddhism flourished, and the Shilla king Munmu built a pleasure garden and summer palace to celebrate the unification. Rare birds and animals wandered through a park whose ponds and hills were landscaped following the principles of Shinson or Taoist philosophy. Kyungju was filled with temples and pagodas, and the most famous temple in Korea, Pulguksa, was built outside the city. 'Kyungju, with almost a million people, was one of the world's largest and richest cities at that time, known and admired as far away as Arabia and India,' says Colin Mason in A Short History of Asia.

It was not to last. Shilla's strict hierarchical system based on ancestry created an elite, and those excluded became discontented, leaving an opportunity for warlords to move in. In 931 the last king of Unified Shilla entertained in his palace the man who would found the succeeding Koryo Kingdom a few years later and move the capital elsewhere. The Shilla palace was abandoned, the site deserted for centuries, and eventually became a habitat for wild birds, leading to its modern name Anapji Pond, anapji meaning 'wild geese'.

Though the city of Kyungju was pillaged over the centuries by the Mongols and the Japanese, they say the spirit of Shilla, the ancient kingdom that built it, lives on today in a 'museum without walls', brimming with national treasures. It's recognised as one of the world's ten most historically significant sites. To get there meant travelling across the country to the south-east in the direction of the East Sea and Japan on my latest solo adventure.

The bus went through the industrial and agricultural heart of the republic. Korea had been for two decades the fastest-growing economy in Asia, though affected by the devastating pan-Asian market crash in the late nineties; it was known for ship-building, car manufacturing, Samsung electronic goods and LG appliances. Here, new roads and apartment blocks were being built, and rows of Hyundai trucks stood ready in rows on red, sandy earth. A mammoth concrete bridge was being constructed over fields of crops, while below, a little farmer was pulling a cart through a shallow stream. I looked up from my book at one point as we crossed the Naktong River outside the industrial town of Kumi. The wide, meandering river looked beautiful in the clear evening light and the lush, blue-green hills were untouched. Darkness fell before the bus stopped at Kyungju.

I walked through the empty streets of the hotel district, while above me the black sky was lit up strangely every few minutes by silent streaks and flashes of lightning. Kyungju being a must-see destination, there was a rather fetid international hostel full of backpackers playing cards. I opted instead for the air-conditioned Chorok-Chang, or Green House, with the usual selection of violent and pornographic videos by the staircase. My room was character-less in typical *yogwan* fashion but cool and clean, with a huge red LED clock of the kind one might find useful in a bus station.

Spotting vertical neon signs down a sidestreet, I went into a bar with a beer garden in the back. Ultraviolet lights zapped insects and a Korean girl sang 'New York Frame of Mind' for a crowd of two. Behind her rose a grassy hillock which I realised, with some excitement, was an ancient Shilla burial mound. Back at the motel, I dismantled the alarm clock to rid the room of its strange LED glow and morbid countdown of minutes, and went to sleep with great hopes for the next day.

In the middle of Kyungju was Tumuli Park: twenty burial mounds of Shilla monarchs, man-made hills constructed up to thirteen metres high. After twenty minutes of walking around its boundary wall towards a ticket booth with souvenir stands and tour buses, I wondered what they meant by 'museum without walls'.

The next important thing to see was the seventh-century Astronomical Observatory Tower, the oldest in Asia, outwardly simple and yet designed intricately with 366 stones, roughly one for each day of the year. Again, there was a fence and a ticket booth. The only advantage of buying the ticket seemed to be that you could get close and have your photo taken next to it, which many people were already doing. Koreans like to have their photo taken beside famous sights. It has its roots in Confucianism; as Simon Winchester says in his book *Korea*, it is important *'to be seen to be doing the right thing* and to have proof of having done it for the elders back home'. I gave it a miss and kept going.

I was dying to see Anapji Pond, the site of the summer palace of Unified Shilla. I left my backpack with the friendly ladies selling souvenirs, walked across the green lawns towards the ornamental ponds, and tried to feel the history of the place. It might have been easier before they built the busy main road that ran around the site. It was pretty, but dull, a backdrop for wedding pictures with no sense of what it once had been.

As the morning progressed in the 'museum without walls', I started to feel the object here was to tick off the sights from your list, take photographs and buy stuff. My mood wasn't much lifted when I reached the museum *within* walls. My big backpack contained the emergency tent as usual and it seemed absurd to carry it around the museum. There were lockers, the guards said, but it turned out they were too small.

'Can't I just hide it in a corner?' Stealing was unheard of here.

'*Aniyo.*' The guards looked sniffily at my short shorts and black trainers, and dismissed me.

They were clearly used to a better class of visitor. It's true that appearances are important in Korea, but it hadn't been a problem before. I carried my bag.

The museum *within* walls, perversely, housed all the fascinating treasure of Anapji Pond – the excavated objects from the ancient summer palace that lay buried underground for so long. The minutiae of everyday life at the palace were here – locks and keys, incense-burners, laundry paddles, hooks for hanging bamboo blinds, silver needles and scissors – along with evidence of civilised aristocratic entertainments such as boats and oars, and delicate ornaments in the shape of lotus flowers. My favourite was a set of oak party-dice, with commands engraved on their sides: roll one, and 'Dance silently'; another, 'Drink and sing'; 'Request anyone to sing'; 'Empty two cups of wine'; and the unforgettable 'Let others hit your nose'. And there were dazzling gold crowns, elaborate but paper-thin, with spangles and pieces of jade shaped like cashew nuts hanging on thin gold strings. Imagine the thrill of unearthing all this.

Encouraged, I headed out by bus towards the famous temple of Pulguksa, the 'Buddha Nation Temple'. I worried, though, when I saw signs with cute cartoon monks pointing the way of the 'tour'. Then I realised one of the great halls, directly behind the Hall of Great Enlightenment, had been transformed into a large gift shop. The temple was overrun with tourists taking photographs. I tried to appreciate the long cloisters and lovely paintings, but I couldn't connect with anything. These places so highly prized seemed to have lost their Buddhist spirit entirely.

I was just sensitive to being on the tourist route. They had chosen to turn their town into a Shilla theme park, with Shilla pharmacies, Shilla petrol stations and family restaurants with Shilla-style curly roofs. Organised travel wasn't working for me. I found the first bus heading out of town towards the sea, anywhere, and bought a ticket to the end of the line.

Travel in Korea has not always been safe. The first European to write about a sojourn in Korea was the Dutchman Hendrik (sometimes spelled Hendrick) Hamel, who arrived in August 1653 when he was shipwrecked in a storm, losing half the crew in fifteen minutes, off the south coast en route from Taiwan to Japan. Once on Korean soil, he found it very difficult to leave: he and his shipmates were held captive for thirteen years. The king in Seoul simply said 'it was not his policy to send foreigners away from his land' – a rather extreme form of hospitality – because he did not want his country to become known to other nations. They communicated through another captive Hollander, Jan Janse Weltevree, who had been in

Korea for almost thirty years, long enough that he hardly remembered his own language.

Korea was by then a 'Hermit Kingdom'. While British explorers like Raleigh, Spanish ones like Antonio de Berrio, the Portuguese and the Dutch had been sailing the world's oceans and laying claim to its lands for a hundred years, Korea kept to itself, barely aware of the outside world. During those years, Korea was repeatedly attacked and invaded by its more aggressive neighbours, Japan and Manchuria. The country had recovered, but developed an understandable fear of other nations, and simply closed its doors.

The Hollanders were held on the southern island of Cheju and treated with friendship by the governor then ruling, but subsequent governors were less kind and the men grew weak from eating nothing but rice or barley flour. Hamel's account describes Chejudo as being highly populated, though poor, and fertile with plenty of horses and cattle. He describes the 'high mountain' (the volcanic Hallasan) and valleys where rice was cultivated. Eventually, they were transferred to Seoul, making the long journey up the west side of the country on horseback, passing through Kongju. In Seoul, the king refused again to let them leave the country, then asked them to perform a little show of dancing and singing, and drafted them as his bodyguards, oddly enough. The Dutchmen were allowed a certain amount of freedom in Seoul, as long as they didn't try to escape. They bought houses and were admired by the Koreans for their fair skin, but they were always looking for a way to get home.

Of the thirty-six survivors from Hamel's ship, the *Sperwer*, only eight escaped finally to Nagasaki, most of them in their late twenties and thirties by then. When they reached Japan, the Korean king's fears were realised: they divulged to their Japanese interrogators how the Korean army was armed (muskets, swords, bow and arrow and some pieces of artillery), where the fortresses were (near every city, usually on a high mountain, with enough food for three years), and how many warships they had (every city had to maintain one). The Japanese also asked what the Dutchmen knew about the land link between Korea and China, and what the purpose of ginseng root was. Then they let them return home.

It was dark and the rain was falling heavily when my bus reached the end of the line at the East Sea, the sea that Hamel and his men had crossed eventually to Japan. We stopped at a town called Kampo that I knew nothing about. I sheltered from the downpour for a while along with other disembarking passengers, then when it looked like the torrential rain wasn't stopping, I walked off into the night in search of a room. Before long, I found a man and a woman to ask if there was somewhere to stay. We conversed in the usual way, with a handful of Korean words, a handful of English, and lots of hand gestures.

'Here is a hotel,' the man said, pointing to the large tower that dominated the view.

I explained that I was hoping for a cheap guesthouse. 'Do you know of a *minbak*?'

They didn't think so. Then they deliberated and invited me to follow them. The man assured me that it was safe: he was the postman. Because of the complicated numbering system in Korean streets, houses being numbered depending on when they are built rather than where they are, postmen are accorded a high level of respect. We walked off through winding streets, and I felt rather gleeful that my way was being guided again. Eventually, we arrived at a house and they introduced me to the lady of perhaps forty who answered the door.

'This lady is Kim Cheung-suk. This is her house. I live upstairs,' said the postman, pointing. He wrote down his address in my notebook. I took off my shoes and sat on a mat on the living room floor, and the postman left shortly after, leaving me with the two women.

Cheung-suk broke the ice by showing me some photographs of herself and her husband on holidays around Korea, and was surprised when I recognised and named the famous places. She asked me how old I was, whether I had a husband, why I was travelling alone. We shared a beer, *maekju*, communicating with some difficulty, and all got a little giggly as she and her friend, curious about my clothes, bizarrely asked me to show them the sports bra I wore under my vest T-shirt. When eventually I thought I'd better start yawning and get to bed, wherever it was, they instead suggested we all go out.

My new girlfriends took me down to the seashore to a brand-new bar in the shape of a ship, where we had more *maekju* and fishy crisps and I tried to expand my Korean vocabulary, although I wasn't likely to remember any of it. The bar was quiet and bright and lacking in atmosphere, but they were proud of this modern establishment in their small town. When finally we went back to the house, Cheung-suk offered me a little room off her living room, where washing was hanging to dry. She lingered in the room as I spread out my sleeping bag. We said goodnight.

I woke around six with sunshine streaming through the window, blue sky above. I hunted around for my socks and shoes near the door and found the outside bathroom. When I returned to my room and sat down on the sleeping bag, Cheung-suk came in and, to my surprise, curled up on the floor next to me like a cat. I felt slightly awkward. I had no idea what to do when your host curls up on your bed. I awkwardly made conversation, showed her my map and explained where I'd been, then decided to go for a walk. My socks had moved again; white hairs gave away that the little pet dog was taking them every time I left them by the door.

Kampo was a proper fishing village, and it smelled fishy, with bags of fishy rubbish lying about. Towards the end of the deserted pebble beach there was a little restaurant set up in tents. Fishermen had hung their wetsuits on a line to dry after coming in with the morning's fresh catch. Just beyond were a military hut and razor-wire fence. This fence extends all down Korea's east coast as a precaution against invasion by the enemy to the north. The west coast is free from it because the beaches there shelve very gradually for a long way out to sea, removing the possibility of a surprise attack by boat.

Back at the town end of the beach, at the harbour, there was much industrious activity as fishing boats unloaded, men and women winding the nets into neat piles as they took out the fish, and others mending nets. In an open warehouse, men and women were packing fish into crates.

Empty crates were hosed down with water, and smoking ice fell down a chute from the upper floor into a cart, to be pressed into the boxes with layers of fresh fish. On the quay, men with slicked-back hair and rubber overalls squatted around an upturned crate on their break, smoking cigarettes and placing bets.

Where the harbour met the village were a dozen raw-fish restaurants, the tanks outside filled with orange crabs with spiny long legs, or purple squid with their pointed hoods, a wild variety of sea creatures. I walked for a while longer, taking photos, then headed back to the house. Cheung-suk was coming up the street in her black sleeveless dress, wearing rubber gloves. Had she been working at the docks? Where was her husband from the photographs? Was he a fisherman, on a trawler at sea perhaps? I wished my language skills were sufficient to get to know more. I felt thrilled to have been invited to stay in her house, and yet utterly foolish for not being able to learn much about her life.

She carried into the living room a low lacquer table covered with bowls. She'd made a delicious lunch of fried fish and seaweed soup and rice, accompanied by side dishes of marinaded greens and pickled vegetables from tupperware boxes in the fridge, and we sat down together and enjoyed the food. I smiled, and she smiled back. As we sat cross-legged on the mat together, she painted my nails with her nail polish, and brought out a wooden Buddhist bead bracelet, and gave it to me.

It was time for me to leave. I wanted to take her photograph, but she was reluctant to let me, complaining she was wearing only her house-dress and no lipstick, with her hair piled in a bun. I persuaded her to allow me to take a picture of her looking natural with her son and the dog. But she also gave me three other formal photographs of her with her husband. In the first they were sitting on a mountain-side on Cheju Island, dressed in their best clothes, on their honeymoon; in the second, he had his hands on her shoulders at Maisan; in the other, he had his arm around her, standing in front of a huge seated Buddha at Soraksan.

I'd found it impossible to experience the true spirit of Buddhism at Kungju, which was full of day-trippers taking photographs. Yet now this complete stranger, Mrs Kim, who any other day might have been one of those day-trippers, had given me the opportunity to experience life in this Korean fishing town. I was so grateful. She was generously exercising her Buddhist principle of offering kindness to strangers, and she now, like me, had the story of spending a funny and intimate day with a woman from the other side of the world.

I always find when travelling it's harder to meet women than men, but I hadn't done badly in Korea. In Kongju, I'd met the information officer at King Muryong's tomb, and the cleaning lady there, and the lady who'd been to Niagara who invited me to join her for lunch. At Sudoksa, I'd met Kim Moon-sim who showed me around the temple. My encounters with women in Seoul had been odd, of course. One night, I was wandering in Itaewon and waiting at the traffic lights when a girl came up and said, 'Buy me drink?' I smiled and shook my head – had I just been propositioned by a prostitute? Another night we'd been out with Gav's band at King Club, and Vinny's Korean girlfriend was with us. She had short bleached hair, and an unusual, urban chic; she was a lot of fun, though she seemed to be kept by a rich man in Japan, who paid for her apartment and bought her the fancy clothes. As we were all sitting around the table, she playfully put her hand up my skirt. Then asked me to come home with her. But that was the madness of Itaewon for you.

There had been powerful queens during the Shilla period. But Hendrik Hamel's account of Korea from 1653 to 1666 includes a section on marital law stating that 'the Koreans treat their women as slaves'. Men then could have as many wives as they could maintain and visit prostitutes too, keeping one wife as his housekeeper and others as a sort of harem. Only men could perform important functions like ancestor worship, and men were seen as the mainstays of financial security. Confucianism ranked the male above the female and created an opporessive social environment for women; the eldest male was the spiritual head of the family, and women existed to serve men and give birth. The only powerful women were mothers-in-law, who were allowed to treat their son's wives as slaves.

When Henry Savage Landor, an eccentric English painter and explorer who often travelled with his kittens, wrote of his months in Korea in the 1890s – an account that is not deemed wholly accurate, it must be said – he was unimpressed by the low status of women, and described the 'very strange custom' that accorded to women the right to walk about the streets of Seoul during the 'woman's hour' after sunset, during which time men were confined indoors but tigers and leopards were on the prowl:

The only privilege she has, as we have just seen, is the chance of being torn to pieces and eaten up by a wild beast when she is out for a constitutional, and that we may safely say is not a privilege to be envied. The poor thing has no name, and when she is born she goes by the vague denomination of "So-and-so's daughter"... The Corean woman is a slave. She is used for pleasure and work. She can neither speak nor make any observations, and never is she allowed to see any man other than her husband.

Isabella Bird, another English writer and traveller, the first woman inducted into the Royal Geographical Society, visited Korea several times between 1890 and 1896. She also attested that 'Korean women are very rigidly secluded, perhaps more absolutely so than the women of any other nation', and wrote of the 'curious arrangement' of men being banished from the streets and women only walking the streets of the capital during the darkest night for a prescribed time. 'A lady of high position told me that she had never seen the streets of Seoul by daylight.' Queen Min, the wife of the twenty-sixth king of Choson, was deemed the most powerful person in the country in the years 1874 to 1895. But royal ladies might never have seen beyond the city walls of Seoul. Not even the royal doctor could set eyes on the queen, while women of lower status were granted much more freedom.

Even in the twentieth century there were 'honour killings' of women for 'sexual shame': there's a horrific story of this in Elizabeth Kim's book *Ten Thousand Sorrows*. The availability of screening technology resulted in that nasty practice of aborting daughters. The exception to all this was the legendary matriarchy of Cheju Island. The women, it is claimed, owned the property, gave the family their name, and only allowed men ashore once a year. Even today in Cheju there are communities of strong fisher-women, who dive to a depth of up to twenty metres, without any breathing apparatus, for seafood or seaweed to sell.

So much changed for women in only a hundred years! In recent years, women throughout South Korea have become successful, even powerful. A major Korean publisher has books on financial planning specifically for women, with interesting titles such as *Women Drinking Starbucks Coffee Vs Women Buying Starbucks Shares*. They are highly educated, and, like western women, their main problems stem from juggling the demands of family and career, trying to get ahead in a traditionally male-dominated society. The women I had met generally seemed friendly and confident.

In Hendrik Hamel's account of seventeenth-century Korea, he wrote that since there were no inns, travellers would be welcomed into private houses for some food and something to drink and a place to stay. Perhaps this was a very old tradition. In any case, taking a bus to the unknown end of the line, to a little fishing village and Kim Cheung-suk's house, had been a good gamble and a worthy detour.

CHAPTER FIFTEEN:

ACQUIRING HAPPY MEMORIES

After Shilla gave way to the Koryo Dynasty, there came a devastating invasion and occupation by the Mongols from the twelfth to the thirteenth century, during Kublai Khan's campaign to subjugate China and Japan. The Choson Dynasty arose from its ashes, founded by one of those who helped drive the Mongols out, the Korean general Yi Songgye, who created the city of Seoul (then called Hanyang).

The emerging Choson society was strictly regimented and controlled and heavily taxed. Koreans had to wear identity tags that indicated rank as well as place and date of birth – very Confucian – and were not allowed to travel outside their home province. The Confucian values promulgated in the Choson era include filial obedience, a hierarchical ranking of family members based mostly on age, and a type of caste system that placed great emphasis on education. These values have, by and large, survived into contemporary Korean society.

In The Red Queen, *Margaret Drabble's novel set in Korea, a character says 'one of the principal weaknesses of our Confucian system was that it made no place for the spirit'. That's where Buddhism was needed to create balance and harmony.*

'I want to go into the sea with you,' demanded my new female friend. 'But I can't swim, so I keep my clothes on.'

Feeling like a day at the beach where I could spend some quiet time reflecting, I'd taken a local bus down the coast from Kampo to Chunchon, trying not to get it confused with Chuncheon. However, quiet time wasn't really on the cards. It was now officially summer, and the beach was filled with teenagers and families. Going for a swim, I felt rather conspicuous. A western woman coming to a beach alone and stripping down to a bikini was a totally bizarre sight to them, and it was hard not to get paranoid. Every time there was a loudspeaker announcement, I imagined it was saying 'Foreigner is entering the water, stand clear!' But after a while people got used to the idea of me being there, and even started saying hello.

I was clearly the only person on the beach interested in getting a tan. Most people went in the sea in shorts and T-shirts, hats and sandals. Every now and then you'd hear someone shrieking as they were thrown into the water fully clothed. It's surprising how many South Koreans can't swim, when the country is almost surrounded by water. For most of the teenagers, the beach was about eating and taking photos.

The water was cool and deep, and though it was a little oily, you could clean off in the shower-*jang*. The people having the most fun of all seemed to be the coach-parties of old folks. Wrinkly ladies would strip down to their waists when changing into dry clothes, and chuckle away at one another's wet T-shirts. Korea seems a good place to be old: a time for playing chess in the park, dancing, picnicking, always in company. It's firmly embedded in Korean culture that you must look after your elders, and those old people who lived through the Korean War and the Japanese occupation certainly deserved a good time now.

Wearing a sarong over my bikini I walked the length of the beach, watching, and on the way back met a young man and woman who insisted I sit with them and share their cans of beer.

'We want you to think well of Korea,' the young man said. The young woman held my hand and fluttered her eyelashes at me, smiling and passing me the beer. This seemed to be the week for meeting interesting women.

'Please have some *ochinga*,' her friend said, handing me the packet of dried squid.

'Thank you. Where are you from?' I asked.

'Taegu,' he said, a big city inland from here. He wrote their address in my notebook. He asked what I was doing in Chunchon, and tried to tell me a Korean expression for the type of travel I was doing. My female friend was getting bored and declared we should go in the water, although she couldn't swim so had to keep her clothes on. I removed my sarong as she grabbed my hand and pulled me in. We splashed around in the waves for a bit, I in a bikini and she in her white shirt and black trousers, and then I got out and took her photograph as she stood, grinning in the water in her soaking clothes. When she emerged, she handed me what she called her 'two-hundred dollar sweater' to dry myself on, and grabbed my sarong to dry her hair.

'I don't mind that I got my expensive clothes wet, I don't mind you wet my two-hundred dollar sweater. I go in the sea with you because you are so beautiful,' she claimed. She was a real comic actress. I reminded her that her friend was throwing her into the sea fully clothed when I'd passed by earlier. She merely pointed to her cheek to ask for a kiss.

'I am very sorry for my English,' she said. Then she dismissed me.

'We can go back to Taegu happy now,' said her friend, 'because we have met you.'

I had set up my tent on the sand among the teenagers and families. Camping was free. As the afternoon wore on, a popular attraction was beach karaoke in an open tent on the sand with the requisite screen and microphone. It seemed rather public for Koreans, who usually did their singing in private rooms. As dusk fell, the guys in the tent next to me lit a campfire and started their own singing. Fireworks started going off everywhere. I liked the fact that young people could set up their tents here for free, set off fireworks, eat and sing safely surrounded by friendly faces. But I craved a bit of peace and solitude.

I wandered off a way to where it was quiet, and sat cross-legged to watch the red moon rising from the sea. Four pale swathes of cloud hung above it like calligraphy; a thin reflection stretched across the water like a pathway of moonlight from the horizon to the shore, cherry coloured, red and yellow. As I sat watching in the dark, a young guy who said he was an off-duty policeman but looked barely old enough – Koreans always looked so young to me – asked if he could sit down. He said he wanted to talk, but the whole conversation consisted of him saying the Korean word for English then drawing a cross on his palm and saying 'No'. I nodded, and concentrated on the moon changing colour and rising up the lines of cloud as if they were rungs of a ladder. Eventually they stretched out to thin lines across a big yellow three-quarter moon.

Leaving behind the policeman but not having the energy to go through the whole raw-fish experience for dinner – it was something that people tended to do in groups, and the food was only sold in big expensive plates – I went for the easy option and bought a cheap pot of quick noodles, *shin ramyun*, from a friendly lady at a beach shop who was putting her young son to bed. She gave me chopsticks and poured hot water from an urn on my plastic bowl of noodles, and directed me to a low lino-covered platform on the sand where I could sit and eat and listen to the waves.

When I woke early the next morning, the sun was already roasting the tent. The beach was completely covered with litter, especially where my campfire neighbours had been singing the night away. A lady came by with tongs and bag to pick it up, piece by piece. I couldn't help thinking it would be better if people didn't leave their rubbish lying about. While I was packing up my tent, the teenage girls in the tent on the other side of mine asked if they could take their photograph with me, insisting we put our arms around one another as friends. The lady who rented out inflatables gave me a thumbs-up sign.

It was almost time to head back to Seoul, but something was urging me to see Kirimsa, a nearby temple. I still craved some reflective, peaceful space. The experience at the commercialised Pulguksa had been so uninspiring; I hoped this less famous place would be different. I started out walking, and within minutes was offered a lift by a man in a van. I was doubly lucky: he was learning English, asked interesting questions, and talked about his kids as he drove. He asked where I was going, where I'd been, and was impressed by my travels but seemed very sad when I admitted that I hadn't made it to see King Munmu's underwater tomb, just down the coast and obviously the big local attraction.

I'd read about it: a legendary tomb of a famous Shilla king buried under the sea, which you could glimpse from the cliff above. Perhaps it's the symbolism that makes it such a prized treasure, because King Munmu ordained his ashes to be scattered at that spot so his spirit would protect the Shilla Kingdom from Japanese pirates. Fed up with sightseeing after Kyungju, I'd decided to give it a miss, but now, not wanting to offend the driver who'd been kind enough to pick me up, I told him I'd run out of time. That was unfortunate, he said, but he added proudly he would drive me there himself next time I came. He drove me all the way to the gates of Kirimsa, where he asked someone to take a photo of us, and earnestly asked me to post him a copy of the photo, giving me his address in Chunchon. Insisting on paying my admission, he wished me happy memories of Korea, and left. I walked up the hill, smiling.

The president recently asked people to be especially nice to visitors in the lead-up to Visit Korea Year. Was it because for so long nobody left Korea with happy memories, and so few people come here to acquire them?

As I walked up the hill towards the temple, there was silence all about except for the quiet tocking of a wooden instrument somewhere. I stopped to read a sign giving Kirimsa's history. Then a class of chattering teenage schoolboys came boisterously up the path and drowned the silence as they showed off, reading from the English sign for my benefit. I grinned, and walked up the pathway ahead of them.

I reached a small courtyard surrounded by wooden meditation halls; in the middle an old tree cast a circular shadow around itself in the midday sun. From a gloomy hall came the monotone of a monk striking a wooden drum, a gong struck in another hall, and a monk in another hall began to sing. The clean sounds merged in a natural harmony. This was what I had been looking for, I knew at once. I sat and immersed myself in its simple beauty.

A temple was first built here by a monk from India who educated 500 disciples. It was enlarged and given its current name in 643 during the reign of the Shilla queen Sondok. Pulguksa, just outside Kyungju, had once been a branch of Kirimsa. Kirimsa thrived in the Koryo Dynasty, and in the Choson era served as a rallying place for troops during the Hideyoshi invasions, the monks becoming a kind of militia. In the Great Hall sat three colossal Buddhas made of clay covered with a smooth, matte gold, the features rather Indian, with pointed noses and heart-shaped faces, and delicate red lines for lips, pale green for the eyebrows and beard. I sketched the patterns carved in the wooden roof-eaves, and fell in love with a hanging painting of a young man carrying radishes on a stick up a mountain to where an old man with a long white beard sat on a tiger.

From the humble wooden buildings to the intricate artwork, Kirimsa had been maintained meticulously, and yet was still a working monastery. Oblivious to the visitors, a group of people sat attentively on the temple floor listening to the monk's teaching. It was a place of worship, study and peace.

I found a hall where the original 500 disciples were depicted in foot-high statues of seated figures, each one individually characterised by a physical attribute or mannerism: one scratching his ear, one pink in the face, one with hairy eyebrows, two slightly overweight, grinning and holding hands. Almost comic, and very human! Were they modelled on the actual disciples? Was each one made by a different monk? As I emerged, pondering this, I saw the group of schoolboys had caught up. There was an excited murmur among the crowd, and the teacher came up to talk to me, explaining that the boys were from a school in Taegu and would like me to be in their group photo. Before I knew it, I was having my photo taken in the centre of an entire class of teenage boys. Each one politely said goodbye as they filed out of the courtyard. Presumably they too could now go back to Taegu with happy memories – and a photo to prove it.

One of the larger halls was dedicated to the reunification of the Korean peninsula. As I examined it, a monk caught my attention and silently mimed eating rice, pointing to the dining hall and signalling to listen for the gong. I was famished, and when the gong sounded I gratefully joined the monks and temple family for one of the best meals I've ever had the good fortune to eat: dark greens with sesame seeds, mushrooms and avocado, flowery stalks, cold soup with seaweed and sesame and cucumber. This food, with its varied textures and tastes, seemed like a celebration of everything that grew on the mountains. A tiny old woman, ninety if she was a day, came over to give me some large green leaves to wrap rice in, and hot green peppers with dipping sauce. Someone else offered sweets and watermelon.

Reluctant as always to leave, I wanted to see the only cave temple in Korea, built in the sixth century by Kwang Yoo and his companion monks from India. This was a few kilometres away. I set off walking, passing friendly ladies sitting in the shade selling herbs and beans and powders for healing, and a coach party of old people lunching under the trees, and creaky old men dancing to the sound of a beaten drum. The valley was filled with swallows and bamboo and rice fields, sun glinting off every leaf. In the blistering heat, though, I was delighted when a bus driver stopped for me.

He kindly gave me a free ride as he wasn't in service, just driving that way anyway, and he dropped me off just down the road. I spotted the gates and made my way up the hill, glad to have a bottle of water.

I saw something high up in the distance on the steep hillside and soon realised that it was the prayer sanctuary of the Stone Buddha Temple. The climb up the rocky cliff was hard but fun with the ropes provided. I met two couples from Taegu, the Korean ladies in their strappy high-heeled sandals managing the climb just as well as me in my rugged shoes. When we reached the cave, the view across the valleys and hills was sublime. This Buddha was known as 'seated at the entrance to Nirvana', and the vista spread out before us was heavenly. I struck up a conversation in English with one of the men as we admired the green forest below, enjoyed the cool breezes and rested. They were on their way to Kampo, and asked about my travels.

'And how do you find the Korean people?'

'Very kind, very warm,' I said.

'Thank you!' they replied. No, thank *you*, I thought. They were thanking me for allowing them to be kind and warm. Sure enough, when we all found ourselves back at the gates, they insisted on giving me a can of ice-cold beer, stuffing a can of apple cider into my bag for my journey, and wishing me happy memories.

CHAPTER SIXTEEN:

HARD ROCK IN THE ROK

In the late sixteenth century there came the invasions from Japan led by Hideyoshi and his samurai army. Recovering from this, Korea once again accepted the dominance of China and agreed to pay it a tribute. Korea clung to China and entered its most pronounced period of deliberate isolationism, learning of the world only through China's contact with it. Korea cut itself off from all other external contact; the Hermit Kingdom did not welcome visiting ships. The royal family of eighteenth-century Choson isolated themselves in the refined palaces of Seoul, rarely leaving the confines of its walls. Respectable upper-class women were supposed to remain indoors.

In 1895, the Korean writer and traveller Yu Gil-jun published his Observations on a Journey to the West, *the first Korean book on such a subject, and wrote what must have seemed completely radical: 'I believe that not only writers and critics but also people of all classes and women as well should know what is going on in the world.'*

The Chinese Empire finally recognised Korean independence at the end of the nineteenth century – but only as a result of pressure from Japan, which was ready to swoop in and take over.

It was always hard to adjust when I got back to Seoul. Coming back after several days away tended to put me in a foul mood temporarily. It was partly something like jet lag: by the time Gav had finished work and we'd relaxed, we tended to go to bed close to dawn, which is when I got up in the countryside. And out there, I'd been hiking and free camping and swimming and meeting people, while back in Seoul I sat around all day, writing in the smoky PC bang, meeting no one and spending too much money on beer. There were days when I hated being back in Seoul, but then I got over it, relaxed and started enjoying it. Although Gav and I still argued sometimes and had misunderstandings, I came back to Seoul each weekend to be with him for his last show of the week, the one night he could completely relax, and his day off.

We were lying in bed on a Sunday, with the fan whirring full blast against the summer humidity, as it had been non-stop all through July. Our frail neighbour was summoning phlegm from the depths of his chest and spitting with gusto, and the strange buzzing insect was buzzing away on the screen window. Feeling far from home, we tortured ourselves by fantasising about cheese and mashed potatoes, about brown toast and baked beans. It started as an innocent 'Wouldn't it be nice to have X for breakfast?' and ended up a long itemising of comfort foods, a Sunday roast with gravy and red wine or real ale. All things you could only have here in synthetic substitutes or for silly money at the international hotels.

It was ridiculous, after such natural feasts as I had had at Kirimsa, and yet it was a nasty trick your body played on you, that you longed for the impossible and after two months in Korea began to daydream of toast and baked beans. It only happened in the city, which to me was not traditionally Korean and yet not western either.

So one morning as we emerged from a night of dancing at Stompers, noticing it was already 6 a.m., we asked the taxi to take us to the Hyatt, and splurged a king's ransom (just for me – Gav got in for free) to shiver in the air-conditioned dining room and gorge on a buffet breakfast of sausages and toast, smoked salmon and croissants. Giggling, I stuffed the miniature jars of jam and honey into my tight jeans pockets on my way out. Later we went to Starbucks at Myungdong for good coffee and cheesecake, sitting on the third floor listening to the jazz muzak while we watched the beautiful people passing below, the shiny, glossy-haired youth of Seoul. We were also tempted into a bar near the Hilton that said it served draft stout; what it actually served was tiny half cans of stout mixed into pitchers of draft OB.

Still, mostly we were loving Korean food. I suggested to Gav we try a little cafe opposite Click and now it was a favourite haunt that we'd dubbed The Kimbap Ladies, where we would have a lunch of *chamchi kimbap*, the rice and seaweed roll made with tinned tuna, or *kyeran ramyun*, instant noodles with egg. We walked to the top of Namsan and decided to have lunch on a restaurant terrace overlooking the city one day. Confidently, I ordered a pork soup. When it arrived, it was so greasy and fatty I couldn't stomach it, and had to remind myself I couldn't be expected to adapt to everything Korean in the space of one summer.

Usually when I was gallivanting around the country, Gav would do the show, then go out to Hollywood and spend time with other musicians. He slept late, went to the Hyatt for a civilised free lunch. Then sometimes he'd watch videos – films or drumming videos – in the afternoon until it was time to get ready again. It was just a normal working week and sounded terribly dull, but he still got a real high from the good nights on stage.

Maybe it was because I kept returning full of amazement and stories, but Gav decided to leave the band at the end of the Seoul contract, so we could travel together. They didn't have another contract lined up – a few possibilities had fallen through – and so if he stayed with them he'd have to go back to Toronto and play in some club in the suburbs. The contract Good Vibes were hoping to get next was playing in a casino in Las Vegas, or on a Disney cruise ship, either of which would be pure misery to him. He joined to see the world. And, I think, he wanted to travel with me, which of course made me happy.

He gave a month's notice to Dean, the band leader, to enable him to line up another drummer, which shouldn't be difficult given that there were so many other bands around, always in flux. Dean said no hard feelings. Gav spoke to another drummer called Chris, from Montreal, who was interested in taking over his position.

The end of July meant the end of the contract at the Hard Rock Cafe for the group from Adelaide. The next Sunday we were invited to their final show in Apkujongdong, which was across the river, one of the most expensive and sophisticated areas of Seoul, full of boutiques with staff who followed you around the shop.

Gav and I went first to a Vietnamese restaurant – new and rather fancy, but we craved the familiar taste. You didn't get Vietnamese immigrants running Vietnamese restaurants in Seoul, it was run by Koreans. The waitress started giggling so much she couldn't even take our order, so the manager took our order of two bowls of *pho ga*. He tried to explain what it was, and we said we'd had it before at home, which he found hard to comprehend given that we were clearly not Vietnamese.

When the *pho ga* arrived, they'd tried to make it more Korean by serving tepid soup in tiny bowls. We were paying an awful lot for this pleasure, so when the manager came over to ask if everything was OK, I asked if we could have it heated up. A few minutes later, a young waiter arrived with two steaming bowls of soup on a tray, obviously nervous as he balanced the edge on our table. Shaking, he carefully lifted off the nearest of the bowls, and the other slid back, tipping the tray and emptying its scalding contents into his lap. Oops. Apkujong wasn't quite the cosmopolitan centre of sophistication it looked, though it was trying hard.

Back outside, we were surprised to see an Irish pub, with a sign in the window saying 'Draught Stout'. 'Orangeman's Day' was a rather unusual name for an Irish pub, but this was Korea after all. The idea of Guinness on tap seemed too much of a taste of home to pass up, and too funny to ignore, given that Gav was Irish and we met in an Irish pub. So we made our way up the stairs, where we found a barman standing over a fridge of cans in an empty room. They didn't have draught stout, he admitted, in fact they didn't have draught anything, not even OB *hof*. But we could buy a small can of Guinness for 20,000 won (US$20). We weren't that desperate, thankfully.

We made our way to the Hard Rock Cafe, where the Australian band Hot Dog were getting ready. Hot Dog seemed an odd name for a band in a country notorious for eating dog. Most Koreans were now embarrassed about the practice and kept dogs as pets, but apparently there were still a few dog meat restaurants; it was believed to be good for the male libido. Dog meat restaurants were extremely rare and very, very expensive, so you never had to worry about eating it by mistake. Perhaps the band's manager should have thought better of using the name Hot Dog in Korea, but it didn't seem to have kept people away.

It was more of a working-class Korean crowd than the international jet-setters of the Hyatt. When the live music started, we joined the Koreans dancing to a Beatles number. One sweet middle-aged couple, both wearing hats, had some very fancy moves. Hot Dog reciprocated culturally by playing a couple of Korean love songs, and Gav was invited up on stage to play drums for a Lenny Kravitz hit. I was very impressed and proud of my rock musician. After the show, we helped Hot Dog pack up their gear. They'd been here for three months and didn't want to leave, so it was lovely to discover the staff had arranged a dinner for them to say thank you, and even nicer to realise we were kindly invited along.

All twenty-odd of us made our way to a nearby restaurant. A long, low table had been set up in a screened-off outside area, and in the balmy night we kicked off our shoes and sat on little mats, feet tucked under our bums. Waitresses emerged with bottles of beer and soju by the armful. There were holes in the table at regular intervals for barbecues, and the waitresses loaded hot coals into them. Then they covered them over with grills, and brought out plates of raw *galbi*, marinated meat, and laid the thin slices onto the grills to sizzle away. This barbecue style of cooking was called *bulgogi*, literally 'fire-meat', usually beef but sometimes pork. Dishes of tofu and kimchi and pickles were also loaded onto the table. Koreans loved to eat in this shared, leisurely, social way and, like family, everyone dipped their chopsticks in the same bowl.

The girl opposite us delicately put a whole soft-shell crab in her mouth, chewed it up then spit out the shell, urging us to do the same. She knocked back soju like it was Diet Coke, while we tried to stick with beer as much as possible. We learned to spoon some bean paste called *samjang* into a fresh lettuce leaf, add a slice of raw garlic, put a bite-sized piece of meat straight off the grill on top and then roll it up and pop it into the mouth to let the flavours explode. Repeat as necessary.

With all of us eating and drinking together, it developed into a splendidly raucous and spirited occasion. A young Korean who called himself Victor started challenging Gav to shots of soju. 'One shot! One shot! Just one shot!' he shouted, and somewhat bafflingly, 'You are my teacher!' They knocked them back, then minutes later Victor made the challenge, 'Teacher! One shot! Just one shot!' and they did it again. Repeat ad nauseam.

At long last, we left the restaurant awash in those telling green bottles, and made for a *norae bang*, a singing room. As we all squashed into a smoky space, people began to wail along to the music. Gav played U2 on the guitar while, on the TV screen, a man sang a love song because his wife had been shot in the head during an aeroplane hijacking. It was all very surreal. In the hallway outside, Victor sat on the floor with his head helplessly between his legs, semi-conscious, a sad victim of trying to drink with an Irishman. I was feeling tired and a little sad and out of place, with all these youngsters doing their thing and Gav at the centre having a grand old time and barely aware of my presence. But I was starting to understand what Korean nightlife was all about.

Shauna, the band's singer, was by now sharing our flat. On the first of August, I came back from my nightly wanderings around town to find her there when she should have been on stage for another couple of hours. Dean had fired her halfway through a set. Gav arrived back straight after the end of the show. When he had asked Dean what he was doing firing Shauna halfway through a set, Dean had fired him too.

The two talked for hours about the general unbearable madness of the workings of Good Vibes under management that could be astute one minute and psycho the next. It was exhausting just hearing about it. Dean, meanwhile, went out drinking tequila all night. In the morning, he called, and Gav talked to him for an hour, calming him down, with the result that both he and Shauna were reinstated. Perhaps Dean realised it would be hard to continue without the drummer and the female lead singer – the hotels insisted on a female lead singer. Gav was leaving Good Vibes at the end of the month anyway, but he preferred to keep working and making money in the meantime.

The bass player's girlfriend, a tiny, freakish American woman with a face like a bird who wore rhinestone sweaters and cowboy boots, was visiting and poking her beak into everything. She rang and enquired in her strange squeaky voice why she hadn't seen me at the Hyatt.

'I've been here a week and I haven't seen you.'

'I don't really like hanging around the Hyatt,' I said.

'You don't like class?'

What a strange, insulting thing to say. I had no answer for her. I'd tried, I really had.

In the evening, when I went all the way down the hill to my favourite *setak*, or laundry, the metal shutters were down. Perhaps the summer holidays were starting. But the builders hadn't taken their holiday yet, it seemed. Across the road I noticed an old house that was demolished only a week before was already being replaced by a new construction: concrete foundations had been poured, boards were up and steel girders were being put in place with impressive speed. Koreans certainly seemed good at this rebuilding business, perhaps understandably given all those palaces and temples that were continually burned down over the centuries.

It took a lot of hard work to rebuild this country after the Korean War. The succession of military leaders in the sixties and seventies focused on economic growth and a move towards modern technology for South Korea, and the dedicated Korean people created a booming economy – in spite of the huge cost required to keep the army on alert in case of attack from the North. Many of the big household-name companies, the 'giants' like Samsung and Hyundai, Lotte and LG, started as small family businesses, building from the ruins of the war. In forty years, the GDP per capita went from the level of the poorer countries of Africa to that of the lesser economies of the European Union.

With the Asian economic crisis in the nineties, even the giant corporations started going bankrupt. But the miracle of the Han, the 'Asian tiger', was created because people were prepared to work long hours to get on. They seemed studious and industrious, and able to endure hardship. I thought about the family that ran the nearest little shop to our flat. They lived in a tiny room adjoining the shop, where sleeping mats were laid out under a mosquito net at night, and the cash was kept in a box under the television. I remembered those people I saw lying asleep in their cars on Namsan, in their shirts and ties, trying to catch a little rest.

I needed to find out how to extend my ninety-day visa. I'd read that it was possible to extend a visitor's visa by ten days, which was all I needed, so I rang Korean Immigration. The woman who answered had limited English, and her directions on how to find the office seemed too vague: go to Omokkyo subway station, take exit six and walk for ten minutes. But what direction, I asked? She didn't understand. I asked if it would be possible to extend the visa, and she said no; when I asked why, she changed her mind and said it cost nothing to extend it for ten days. Then, bizarrely, a male voice came on the line and said that this phone line had to be shared among ten people and that I should come to the office instead – and he hung up. *Argh. Get me out of Seoul, get me to some peaceful, welcoming country place where people are kind.*

I'd been getting the impression that this first week of August might be prime summer holiday week, but it hadn't occurred to me what that meant until I got to the bus station. It was heaving with people like Heathrow Airport during a summer holiday strike, and the Excellent Express buses going across the country to the east coast, where I had hoped to go, were booked up for most of the day. Seeing that traffic was going to be heavy anywhere, I decided against a long journey and opted instead for a coastal national park, Taean Haean, which was just a couple of hours down the west coast and yet not far from Toksan, the serene place where I was welcomed into my first Buddhist monastery.

CHAPTER SEVENTEEN:

THE BEACH, KOREAN STYLE

The Japanese occupation of Korea lasted until 1945, and the division of Korea was made as part of the Japanese surrender procedures after the dropping of the atomic bombs on Hiroshima and Nagasaki. During the night of 10 August 1945, two US colonels in the Pentagon chose the thirty-eighth parallel as a simple demarcation line to show where the US zone would end and the Russian zone begin. This separated the mostly agricultural south from the more industrial north. The Soviet military then sealed off their zone and stopped trade and traffic with the south. The Allies attempted to re-unify Korea until December that year, but the Soviets refused to consult with Koreans who disagreed with the proposed trustee government system. So two separate governments were created.

The Soviets installed as leader a man who had been a communist partisan plotting against Japanese rule from outside the country — Kim

Il-sung. He conferred with Stalin about how to proceed, discussed what support he could expect. Just as the US was beginning to turn its attention elsewhere, the North attacked in the middle of the night on 25 June 1950, starting a war that would achieve nothing but destruction and shut down the border completely.

'This time, once past, will never more return,' said Dong-kyuen, a thirty-something man from Seoul with an extraordinary command of English that made it sound like romantic poetry.

I sipped on my lukewarm beer and thought that this eloquently encapsulated fact did not distress me greatly. I had by now sampled the entertainment possibilities of Mongsanpo that evening, where thousands of Koreans had gathered to camp by the Yellow Sea. I'd eaten noodles, watched the performance of mediocre pop bands on stage, and inspected the rifle ranges. The tide was out about half a mile and the muddy wet sand was alive with hundreds of torches that looked like fireflies in the foggy gloom – people digging for crabs.

Somewhat improbably, considering the masses that thronged this seaside camp, Dong-kyuen was feeling lonely. Having convinced me to come and drink beer with him, he ordered several big bottles at a time so they sat on the table warming up, and gassy OB does not improve at that temperature. He was paying, however, so I couldn't complain, and he also ordered a big plate of fruit. And he spoke English. So I sat and picked at slices of melon and banana while listening to his tales of ten years in the re-insurance business before he left to manage an English language school.

I had actually bought a bus ticket for a place called Mallipo, or Manripo. It's confusing the way anglicised Korean names can be spelt a number of alternative ways. Mallipo can be Manlipo or Manripo, Chongno can be Jongro. Obviously it's because there aren't exact equivalents for our letters in the Korean language, and that old cliché of mixing up 'l' and 'r' happens constantly. There was a funny map outside the Hilton hotel on Namsan, which pointed out the great landmark of the 'Seoul Towel'. In *Welcome to Korea* magazine, an article expressed Seoul's great excitement over the arrival of the famous musical from New York and London, 'Lent'.

Once beyond the shock of ugly pink apartment buildings that was the suburbs of Seoul, the bus drove past racing-green hills, carpets of red chilli peppers laid out to dry in the sun, flat green rice fields parted by a ramrod straight white path where a lone cyclist meandered, white egrets rising from shallow rivers. We passed dusty low farm buildings with curly roofs, apple farms. It was promising.

When I arrived in Mallipo/Manripo, it was packed with cars, people, pounding music, arcade games, greasy smells. It certainly wasn't all bad, as seaside resorts go – there were windswept pine trees on gentle hills, soft sand and beachside shellfish restaurants – but there was barely enough space to pitch a tent on the beach. I thought it might be worth trying somewhere else close by. A nice man in the little bus station advised me how to get further down the coast, and let me use the office phone while I avoided the eyes of the naked models on his calendar on the wall. The bus was full, standing room only; as it eased into the heavy traffic, one woman kindly offered me the edge of her seat as a perch, and another gave me a stick of chewing gum. There was no getting over how kind people were.

It was dark when I arrived, and hard to see how far the campsites stretched beneath pine trees – but it looked like kilometres. On an enormous music stage, Korean teenage musicians were approximating heavy rock ballads. Mongsanpo was like a small town, with streets of restaurant tents and amusement tents and karaoke tents, even PC bang or computer gaming room tents. There were fireworks exploding all over the beach, and kids jumping up and down in trampoline tents. Finally I managed to find a space down a back-alley under my own pine tree. I laughed grimly, thinking of my mother's email reminding me not to camp anywhere too remote. The quiet beaches I'd visited before had clearly been an out-of-season aberration. These people's idea of fun was sharing your bit of seaside with masses of others. It wasn't quite what I'd expected.

Dong, my new friend, who was a little overweight and dressed in casual clothes, told me he was here alone and happy to find some company since he'd been feeling very solitary. Amazed, I asked if he didn't find it a little, um, crowded? He said this was quite peaceful compared to some places. Koreans only take five days holiday a year, he said, all at the same time. We should seize the moment and enjoy the fact we've found some company. 'This time, once past,' he reminded me, 'will never more return!' And he quoted something from Plato. You had to give the guy credit.

Dong was right in a way: this beach-themed extravaganza wasn't a place to visit on your own, it was a place to come with company. For me, travelling alone had been absolutely the best way to be welcomed into Korea. But I was learning that unless you were a monk, Koreans saw it as a sad thing to be alone, *honja*. To be happy, you must have company. That's why food was best when you shared it, all eating from the same dish in the middle of the table. That's why people liked travelling in groups. I found the same thing when I lived in Greece, where my friends would always like to do things with company; in Syntagma Square one day, an older woman ignored every other empty bench in the square and sat right up next to me. Sometimes I wished I didn't need my personal space. I'd have been having a better time in Mongsanpo.

Dong kept ordering and we sat around until after midnight. After a few more beers, he mistakenly mentioned his sister and her kids were here somewhere. I sensed he had been exaggerating the truth of his loneliness somewhat and, with some surprise, couldn't help being flattered that in this country where I had felt so foreign and asexual for ages, someone was seriously trying to pick me up. In the end, he was quite hard to shake off, getting all romantic as he walked me back to my tent, lunging in for a kiss before I could scamper off and zip myself into safety.

Next morning was cool, cloudy and wet, and the tide out so far you could barely see the water. A loud argument seemed to be going on in the next tent. The toilets I'd found so far all smelled vile, and I queued for ten minutes only to find vomit-covered sinks and no running water.

It was like being at a rock festival. I felt dirty. I wanted a swim, but tired of walking on mud through inches of water looking for the sea. The rubbish ladies hadn't been round to clean up yet, and I was reminded of how much I hated this habit of leaving rubbish on the beach. Everyone else was out with buckets and spades, digging for crabs.

Wandering this vast beach-metropolis once more, I saw that everyone else was having a great old time. Seoul had come to the beach, and while Seoul-on-sea was a hoot for these folk, I was floundering in its indifference. While I wanted to connect with Koreans, going on holiday with thousands of them didn't seem to be the best way. I'd reached a dead end. I packed up to move on.

I stopped for pork dumplings that tasted of the plastic packaging they were microwaved and served in. I started walking to the next beach but saw more mud and a discouraging sign saying 'Experiment Station'. So instead I stood at the bus stop with three ancient crones. Eventually a bus came along and I noted with glee that the driver was nattily sporting white cotton gloves, sandals and socks with individual toe-pockets; I felt better already. We made our way into the traffic jam that was the road back towards town. It started to rain lightly. The farmland was lovely and green, pines dripping with water. I could come back here another time.

I rang Gav from the Taean bus station, while the rain poured down outside. 'I know a place in Seoul you can stay,' he said. We spent a happy, lazy afternoon at home, Gav strumming a guitar he'd borrowed and singing to me.

In Seoul, the workers at the Lotte Hotel were demanding a pay increase, and beside their peaceful demonstration we saw hundreds of black-uniformed riot police with helmets, shields and batons.

It was an eerie reminder of the kind of fascist regime that existed here before democracy arrived. Kim Dae-jung's was the first administration to be liberal about ideological matters. The first strikes by workers demanding better wages from the giant corporations, which took place in the late eighties, turned into riots. When students, office workers and Buddhist monks demonstrated against the undemocratic elections of 1988, the authorities met them with riot police, tear gas and mass arrests. It was, therefore, extremely discomforting to see so many riot police today.

I saw them again another day: more ranks of police, lines and lines of them, filing down into the tunnels of the subway. The expressionless faces of young men with guns and batons were frightening. I discovered that the biggest anti-US demonstrations since President Kim Dae-jung took office had been happening. Thousands of protesters had accused the government of kow-towing to Washington, allowing US troops to pollute their land and opening up the country to cheap agricultural imports.

Trainee doctors were also on strike across the country, protesting a medical reform programme. Interns and residents were dissatisfied with their working conditions and salaries, so the government was threatening to fire them and send them off to do their military service, which they were excused during training. A rally had been suppressed, the leaders arrested.

What was so hard to understand was that all this was going on while such a poignant moment was happening in Korea: the family reunions between North and South.

For fifty years after the country was divided, there was absolutely no contact between families separated by the division of the country – no telephone calls, no letters – except in 1985, when fifty people from each side were allowed to visit Seoul and Pyongyang. An estimated ten million people are members of divided families, and many don't even know if their relatives are alive. The Asian Bureau chief for the *Boston Globe*, Indira Lakshmanan, compared it to the division between East and West Germany, saying that at least families were allowed to write letters, make calls and send packages across the Berlin Wall, all of which has been forbidden in Korea. In *House of the Winds*, a novel by Korean-American Mia Yun set in the sixties, an old woman tells how she spends her days waiting and hoping that one day she will be able to go back home to the North. 'I'm afraid I'll die without ever seeing my family and home again… The river, the hill and the village: I remember everything…'

For four days in August 2000, in Seoul and Pyongyang, people were being reunited briefly with loved ones from whom they had been separated for half a century, with no way of knowing if they'd ever meet again.

The newspapers were full of heart-rending photographs and stories of mothers, fathers, brothers and sisters reunited. A man in his sixties met his mother who was in her eighties.

'I feel sadder than when we first met,' he said. One hundred North Koreans – a drama writer for the North Korean Central Broadcasting Station, a painter – were in Seoul. And from 76,000 people who applied, one hundred South Koreans were selected for the reunion in Pyongyang. These were tearful, painful reunions, and they were taking place under strict rules, highly controlled formal meetings within big hotels, with no one allowed to visit their home town. The hundred individuals from North Korea who came to the South were only allowed to meet five of their family members. One lady who was the sixth stood by the hotel where her brother was; when he was escorted out, she screamed, 'Older brother!' But he wasn't allowed to step out of line to greet his youngest sister.

The thawing of relations between the two Koreas brought hope. The South agreed to repatriate sixty former communists who served prison sentences here, and the two Koreas planned to hold Red Cross talks about the separated families.

It was finally time for Gav and me to visit the most amusingly named Irish pub in the world, O'Kim's. Alas, it was a big room of tables, nobody making friends, nothing like an Irish pub. Craving Guinness, we instead visited the plush bar at the Hilton and paid an outrageous sum for a couple of pints served with olives. Having had enough of its pesky zzz, ZZZ, ZZZZZ – heh heh heh, Gav killed the wind-up bug on the screen window, having the last laugh.

On the Sunday we spent an afternoon at the lively and completely western Gecko Lounge in Itaewon, spending another small fortune on pitchers of beer and dancing to 'Home for a Rest' by Spirit of the West, funnily enough. Somewhere into our second pitcher of beer they played 'Paradise by the Dashboard Light' by Meatloaf and I expounded a lengthy thesis on what a brilliant song it was and how much it said about being a teenager... Gav listened and nodded, grinning, as I'd probably have forgotten it all by the next day. When we first met, he refused to let me have an opinion on music, saying he was a musician and knew better. All because I didn't like The Police. He talked about songs in terms of chord progressions and notes, while for me it was all about the lyrics, the words, and he now at least let me have my say.

The American editor of the Weekender section of the *Korea Herald* said he was definitely interested in pieces I wrote on the fortress at Suwon and on hiking in the mountains and national parks. I was thrilled. They needed photos for both.

I could get to Suwon in an afternoon by train. I left Seoul so late that by the time I arrived I only had a couple of hours before dusk, but was happy to stop and talk with a young man who worked as a part-time tour guide, though he was actually a criminology and jurisprudence student. He gave me a book about Suwon and a cold drink of water, and told me how the city walls were constructed with both bricks and stones for strength, and about the advanced use of cranes and pulleys. As he answered a couple of questions for me, we sat in his hut where he was playing a tape of Korean classical singing on the stereo. It was beautiful music, and I asked about the name of the artist. He took out the tape and I started to copy down the name, until I realised he was insisting I take it.

As I rushed around the walls, everyone was out enjoying the evening, sitting in the park or by the river, playing chess or napping. In the setting sun, I watched a white crane fly overhead with outstretched wings, feet straight out behind him. An old man stopped to shake hands with me.

I hurriedly developed the film and dropped it off at the newspaper offices so they could run the story that week, but I still needed some photos to accompany my story on hiking for the following week. They wanted some pictures of Korean walkers. So, armed with a camera, I headed out of town to find some.

CHAPTER EIGHTEEN:

KOREAN MEN BEHAVING BADLY

Popchusa, founded in 553 as a sanctuary to pray for the unification of the three kingdoms that divided the peninsula then, once had seventy hermitages and a gilt bronze Maitreya Buddha where people could pray for national harmony. The temple was burned down during the Hideyoshi invasions and then rebuilt. The bronze Buddha was melted down in the late nineteenth century to mint coins so the prince regent could raise money to construct Kyungbokkung, the palace in Seoul. A cement replacement was begun in 1939 but 'after interruption due to social instability', a nice euphemism for the Korean War on the sign outside, it was completed only in 1964, when it began to erode and crack. The casting of the new figure that stands there today took six years and 160 tons of bronze. Which only goes to show again the importance of symbols of unification and harmony in Korea.

The temple is set in Songnisan, a national park in the Sobaek Mountains, the highest peak of which is just over 1,000 metres high. It was known from ancient times as one of the eight scenic wonders of Korea, and made into a national park in 1970.

I took the bus to Songnisan from the Nambu bus station, where they confusingly spelled it 'Sokrisan'. A girl of about nineteen sitting across the aisle from me in gigantically pointed shoes with high stiletto heels spent fifteen minutes looking into a hand mirror, touching up her face powder and lip gloss. Mostly everyone else got off the bus at a place called Cheongju – confusingly, there was also a town called Chungju close by – which was surrounded by modern hotels in a fantasy-castle style with Disneyland turrets. While we were stopped, a woman with cotton gloves and a bucket boarded the bus to pick up the rubbish and mop the floor. After Mongsanpo, it was a relief to be heading where everyone else wasn't.

From Cheongju the now quiet bus drove past forest-covered mountains as we meandered into the heart of the country. The dark pines were tinged by a sunset that was yellow and then pink, reflected in the flat and gleaming river with its egrets and herons. Our route wound past villages and farms, apple trees and red pepper bushes and crops wrapped in bunches and stacked to dry in the fields. Finally, as it grew dark, the road zigzagged up a steep hill, and I was half frozen from the air conditioning by the time we reached Songnisan. As I emerged gratefully into the warm evening, a woman offered me a cheap *minbak* room, but I decided to camp. The campground when I found it was in complete darkness and I could see only one other tent. I set up mine quickly, hoping I wasn't being bitten by mosquitoes.

The tourist village of restaurants, *minbak* and souvenir shops was strangely deserted. It was only the middle of August, but already the holidays seemed to be over. Dong must have been right about everyone taking a week's holiday at the same time. Avoiding the fancier restaurants, I found a nice traditional sort of place off the main street, where I sat on a wooden mat at a low table. On one side of me, a silent couple picked at their food very slowly; on the other was a bigger group, among whom a man with a very loud voice was holding court with a monologue punctuated with '*kurigo… kurigo…*', roughly translating as 'And another thing…'. I ate a 'mountain *bibimbap*', *sanche pibimbap*, with mushrooms and beansprouts, served with a cold cucumber and carrot soup and a side dish of peanuts in a sweet soy sauce. Back to lovely country food.

It was cool and pitch black except for a few stars. A large, bright moon rose in the clear sky, so I could see the shape of the mountains all around. I strolled by the river in the moonlight, under big old trees with bent trunks, until I was tired enough to sleep.

It was lovely waking up to a cold dawn in the woods to the sound of only the birds and the bugs. There was a wind-up bug somewhere nearby, going nuts: zwiw, zwiiw, ZWIW,

ZWIIIIIW, heh heh heh heh... But it didn't sound bad here. I wasn't sure if I had camped in the proper campground, but I'd had this place virtually to myself. I consulted the information map, jotting down notes about peaks or waterfalls to head for, and set out along a clear river with a sandy bottom and little fish swimming in it, bordered by Buddhist piles of pinkish stones.

Instead of wandering aimlessly as usual, this time I had a purpose: to reach a mountain peak to take photographs of walkers in a dramatic setting for the *Herald*. Songnisan had clear streams and mushrooms growing, huge stone statues of turtles hewn out of pinkish boulders overgrown with bright green moss – but also, at this time of year, excessive humidity, a profusion of mosquitoes, slippery rocks and cloudy weather. I spent many hours walking up damp paths covered with lush greenery, trying to reach a high peak. But after carrying my heavy backpack in the humid day, my legs were so tired that I couldn't tread carefully and worried I might slip and break my ankle. I really should have been properly organised, taken a room and left my bag in it for the day. The path was overgrown, and I wondered if I'd missed a sign saying the trail was currently closed, as there were no other walkers. I had to turn back defeated, and tried to reach a lower peak, but it was an unrewarding slog through endless trees and rocks, rocks and trees, with no photogenic views to be had. The rain began to come down, making the path even more treacherous, just as my legs were ready to give up. I started back down the hill.

In a little hut, a young man gave me a drink of some spicy cold tea. I bathed my feet in a cold stream, and decided to go back to the start of the trail and visit the temple instead.

Wow, that's a big Buddha, I thought as I rounded the corner. Thirty-three metres tall, to be precise. In the museum that was underneath the platform of the extremely big Buddha, I found delicate and beautiful paintings of kings with long Fu Manchu moustaches and smiling pursed lips, carrying fans in their manicured hands. I noticed the monks and nuns kept their rubber slippers for wet weather in numbered shelves at the entrance to the temple. A prayer session seemed to be beginning, as the monks in grey robes and brown shawls all scurried off to their halls carrying Buddhist objects, to chant and hit their wooden gongs.

Towards the end of the afternoon I started walking back towards the village and said hello to the man on the temple souvenir stand who had given me directions early in the morning when I'd passed by. He was so surprised to see me only just returning, eight hours later, that he gave me a pack of postcards as a gift. He spoke very good English, and explained to me what was on each of the postcards, giving me much more information than I'd been able to glean before from the stilted English on the signs. He explained how the lotus symbolised the Buddhist heart, the flowering of a soul, and that there were many fascinating connections to be made between Buddhism and Christianity – the Buddhist Maitreya is the equivalent of the Christian Messiah, and the Indian word *ohm* is used in the same way as the Christian amen.

This inspiring encounter made my day. It seemed much more important than my intended mission. I bought a couple of Buddhist wooden necklaces, inscribed wooden blocks threaded on fine brown string, thinking to repay him for what he'd taught me, but he insisted on giving me a discount of one-third of the price, presumably all his profit, and labelled the packages carefully for me after I explained which was for my brother and which for my boyfriend. He said he understood that travelling for a long time means not making money, and therefore he realised I probably didn't have much to spare.

I had just left the company of this generous, interesting man and was continuing on my way back to the village when I spotted two older men walking towards me in in full hiking regalia: khaki trousers tucked into colourful hiking socks, walking sticks with built-in functions, and short-sleeved plaid shirts under sporty waistcoats with countless pockets. The older of the two, trim with grey-white hair, also sported a bandanna tied neatly around his neck, and natty white cotton gloves to keep his hands dry. I thought immediately of the photographs I was supposed to be taking of typical Korean hikers for the *Herald*. They would make an ideal picture as they strolled along, but I didn't want to snap a photo of complete strangers without their permission. So I asked, and they readily agreed.

They posed in a practised manner together, chin out and head held high, hats and walking sticks at rakish angles, then insisted on each having their photo taken with me. We ended up with plenty of photos. They introduced themselves politely. Kim Wook-hyuon, or Wook as he said I should call him, was distinguished-looking, with dark hair, slightly protruding ears and a bit of a paunch. He spoke excellent English with great enthusiasm, having worked some years as an interpreter. He introduced Pyo Jae-suk, or Jae, as his 'older brother', then explained.

'We have been friends for twenty years or so!' He pronounced it *ah-so!* 'I like him because he is always candid and direct. Even when he is lying, he lies directly!' Nice one.

Jae, who spoke little English, was a retired athlete and physical education teacher, with twinkling eyes and a mellow smile. The two had left their families behind in Seoul for a few days of recreation. They searched for something to give me as a present, to thank me for choosing to take their photograph. Jae looked in his knapsack and presented me with his own bamboo fan, demonstrating with a theatrical flourish how to use it. Fans were popular in the heat and humidity of late summer. I protested that I couldn't take his fan, but he insisted happily that I must have it. Wook wrote down their names and addresses in my notebook.

We talked in good spirits for a while and then took our leave. But shortly after, we happened upon each other again near the bus station, where I was looking for a place to stay, and Wook took the opportunity to invite me to spend the evening with the two of them in his little country house, so I could experience real, rural Korean life.

'It is very poor, *very poor,* but I will be honoured if you stay at my house.'

I was not fit to be taken anywhere, having camped out the previous night, not had a shower, then hiked up mountains all this hot day. My clothes were covered more than ever in salt stains from sweating in the humidity. These two men were dressed for hiking, but immaculate, with not a stain or mud spatter in sight. I thanked them but declined. Wook insisted it would be no trouble, however, and at last I couldn't resist the opportunity. There are few places in the world where a woman would feel comfortable accompanying two strange men to a house goodness-knows-where, but Korea felt like one. If I'd taken that *minbak* room and the practical option the night before, I wouldn't have been looking for a place to stay and would never have got this chance. I should take it.

Soon thereafter I was boarding an icily air-conditioned bus with my two new companions. Our journey took an hour, with a change of buses at Miwon, where an amiable man who looked forty-five but claimed to be seventy told me in an American accent that he had served in the Korean War. When we reached Undugmal, Wook's village, it was dark and quiet, and there was a velvety black sky above, full of stars.

We walked past dusty farms, some with curly tiled roofs, and there was a pleasant farmyard smell and only darkness beyond. When we reached Wook's house, however, it was hardly the rustic hovel I was led to expect, but a flat-roofed bungalow with a lily pond and pretty cast-iron lawn chairs. Wook was fastidiously clean and tidy, and everything was in its place. He ordered me to go and take a cool shower, bossily making me stay in the bathroom as long as possible to make the most of the cold water; it was seen as one of the benefits of being in the country during the humid Korean summer, and Wook talked proudly about how cool the water was here. The bathroom had a proper bath and all mod cons. Meanwhile he and Jae cooked up a bachelors' dinner of tuna, steak and eggs, all with Korean touches.

He and Jae had got to know one another when they both taught at the same school, Wook teaching history while Jae taught physical education. Over dinner Wook told me that this was his father's house, where he grew up, though he'd lived in Seoul for over forty years, and he and his wife had travelled all over the world, from New Zealand to Italy to Vietnam. He said he would be honoured for me to visit his house in Seoul also – if his wife would allow it.

'I love my wife, more than anyone else. But… *I am scared of her.*'

In a Korean family, the wife is in charge of the home, which was perhaps why Wook needed to get away from time to time. He showed me photographs. His two 'obedient' sons still lived at home, though both had good jobs in finance. I knew that the younger family members were supposed to obey their elders, though it still sounded unusual to hear a father talk proudly about his grown-up sons as being 'obedient'. But obedient children are doted upon, not repressed. His good-looking thirty-year-old daughter was married.

'Her husband is very intelligent and very kind to me and my wife. In Korea, a daughter is very important. She is my only daughter. I like and love my daughter. I am her slave!'

He asked about my plans for tomorrow. I had planned to go to Tanyang where there was a scenic lake with rocky islands, but he advised against it at this time of year, although it was his favourite place, because the water levels would be too low still. You had to see a place at the right time of year, naturally. We would decide tomorrow. In the meantime, he showed me to the bedroom, which would be mine: he and Jae would sleep on the living room floor. A traditional Korean bed, it was simply a reed mat on the floor with a thin cotton quilt, the reed mat being there to keep you dry in the summer. I was very happy to be getting used to sleeping on the floor, though my limbs had a tendency to lose feeling sometimes. The whole place was spotlessly clean and tidy.

'I am very proud,' said Wook. 'You are the first foreigner to sleep in this room. I hope you will have happy memories of Korea.'

I went to bed, and heard Wook and Jae next door clinking soju glasses together til late in the night. I reflected on the things like this that had been happening to me all over Korea, outside Seoul. Sometimes I felt like a guest of the entire Korean people: at Kirimsa, of the man who promised to drive me personally to King Munmu's underwater tomb next time; in Kampo, of the woman who invited me into her house though we could barely communicate, gave me photographs and her wooden Buddhist bracelet; at the cave hermitage of Kolgulsa, of the day-tripper from Taegu who stuffed ice-cold drinks into my bag. And earlier that day, the souvenir seller had done everything he could to make me remember my time at Popchusa well. I remembered that very first moment of kindness, when the man looking after King Muryong's tomb allowed me inside. In other places, his motives might have been different, but in Korea I was certain he'd given me that opportunity because of pride in his culture.

People had come to my rescue and helped me constantly, perhaps partly because I was traveling *honja*. The discipline, obedience, orderliness and etiquette of Confucianism was more than balanced by the Korean people's natural exuberance, their love of life and their country, and the unstoppable generosity and hospitality of the Buddhist spirit. They were a tight-knit family, but not unwilling to draw you in and make you a friend. I was acquiring very happy memories of Korea.

I woke in the morning to sounds of throat-clearing in the next room, and moving of glasses and bottles from the late rounds of soju. While Wook was tidying up, I had a shower and took a walk outside, where the sun was shining over a valley of farms, surrounded by craggy racing-green hills. Wook had said the previous night that my boyfriend and I were welcome to come to stay at his house, and I imagined how beautiful it would be to sit on the flat rooftop, reading in the sun, in this stillness. When I got back to the house, Wook showed me his garden planted with flowers, and the carp swimming in the pond.

I could smell breakfast cooking. Wook invited me to sit down, and a familiar green bottle appeared, and three shot glasses. Soju, with that sickly smell that was hard to forget long after you'd vowed never again to partake. When it was offered, with the formal gesture of outstretched hands, it was rude to refuse. But for breakfast? Protesting, I was allowed to toast the day with just a small measure, and it did whet the appetite. Wook had cooked up a hearty meal of leftovers, including a *twenjang* or bean paste stew with tiny fish and turnip and hot green peppers. He and Jae showed me how to wrap a crisp, salty square of dark-green dried *kim* around a mouthful of sticky rice using my chopsticks.

Since the day was clear and sunny, Wook and Jae had decided to delay their return to Seoul in order to show me the nearby Hwayang Valley, an area of outstanding natural beauty. They'd been there just the other day, but wanted me to see it. I must have heard of it, Wook said. When I said I hadn't, he looked at me astonished, as if wondering where I went to school.

'It is *very famous*,' he said, 'with Koreans *and* with foreigners.'

I smiled sheepishly. That was decided then – we must go to Hwayang. Wook unfolded a handwritten copy of a bus schedule from his shirt pocket, explaining that his son used his car in Seoul. By the time he'd deciphered his timetable, however, we were late for the bus, and had to make a mad dash through the flat, lush valley. Our huffing and panting was the only sound in the stillness. We waited a few seconds for the bus beside a magic carpet of hot red chilli peppers drying in the sun. These peppers, so vital now to the national dish of kimchi, were only introduced in the late sixteenth or early seventeenth century by Portuguese traders who brought them from Central America – before Korea had quite become the Hermit Kingdom, perhaps, or did they come via China? Occasionally outsiders had brought good things to Korea.

At the Hwayang Valley, steep white cliffs towered over a clear sandy-bottomed river, strewn with massive boulders and overhung with shady trees. We made an unlikely threesome as we hit the trail. Jae walked apart, as he liked to be alone, apparently. According to Wook, he was once a famous basketball player, tennis player and *ssirum* wrestler – the Korean equivalent of sumo – though he certainly didn't have a sumo build. Meanwhile, Wook walked with me and giggled that he felt like a country bumpkin, not wearing socks, his shirt untucked, and carrying a plastic bag filled with *getnip* leaves and peppers that he picked from the country garden to take back to the city. I, however, certainly felt the odd one out. I was feeling rather lithe and tanned from all my hiking, but somewhat gangly in my short army-green shorts, and awkwardly carrying an enormous green backpack.

Hwayang, it turned out, was not only green pools and dramatic rocks. It was the site of a prestigious and renowned Confucian shrine and private academy, Hwayangsowonji, created in 1696 to honour outstanding scholars. Confucian academies were the main centres of learning of the Choson Dynasty, and the Confucian scholars who emerged from them became exceedingly powerful politically. By the eighteenth century there were more than six hundred such academies across the country, even more than in China. The monarchy grew tired of their dominance, however, and began to shut them down. Hwayang was closed because overbearing scholars were collecting excessive tithes for memorial rites, and most of the buildings were demolished.

Signs indicated, in the typical way, which areas were of outstanding beauty and worth viewing or having your picture taken in, such as a lake of golden sand and picturesque cliffs. We walked around, admiring, and finally reached a wooden library built on a rock overlooking the river, where a great statesman once retired to read the classics. There we stopped to bathe in the designated swimming section of the placid river; the other parts of the river were closed to swimmers to keep them clean. Jae warned me that the water where it rushed through the rocks was deep and dangerous. Then he saw that I knew how to swim, and relaxed, rather impressed. We sat at a table and had cold refreshments while taking another set of photographs, Jae and Wook sitting up straight for the camera and looking serious.

We took the bus to Cheongju, from where they could go to Seoul and I could go to Tanyang for another day of exploring, even though Wook had advised against it. Wook had other ideas.

'Whenever I leave or return to my house, I feel hungry,' he said, with a glint in his eye. 'It is *very strange*.' I imagined his wife kept him on a diet at home. Not for the first time, I noticed what a sly sense of humour Koreans have, and how much I liked it. So he led the way to his favourite restaurant, where we sat down shoe-less and cross-legged at a low table.

The *ajumma* (the woman in charge of the restaurant) prepared the *bulgogi* pit in our table and brought side dishes. While slender morsels of beef sizzled on a grill over hot coals in front of us, two bottles of soju arrived, and the toasts began again. According to Korean etiquette, Wook explained, he must not refuse when his senior, Jae, offered him a drink. This was done formally by holding the glass in one hand, and touching underneath the forearm with the other. Exchanging glasses was also an important sign of friendship, so Jae must not refuse if his friend offered him a drink; he must take it, and fill another for Wook. And so it went, Wook and Jae getting gradually louder, rowdier and in better and better spirits. I seemed to be the only one eating. The meat, freshly grilled and wrapped in leaves with garlic cloves and bean paste, was delicious. Wook and Jae urged me to keep eating, while they kept drinking.

'I am his good friend,' said Wook, pointing to Jae. 'His other friend is soju!'

I was relieved to learn that 'according to Korean etiquette, it is not good for men and women to exchange soju'. This rule fell by the wayside at some point, however, and I was urged to join in the toasts. I'd certainly been welcomed into the party. Then, with a triumphant gesture, Jae produced a tupperware jug from his knapsack: home-brewed wine, which his wife made as a present for Wook for inviting Jae to stay with him in the country. The smooth, honey-gold liquid was considerably more palatable than soju, though just as strong. Half the jug disappeared in no time. Dipping into his pack again, Jae, in excellent spirits, produced a small silver case; he removed an acupuncture needle and stuck it into his hand to demonstrate. I assured him I was feeling very healthy.

Drinking has been part of the social fabric of Korean life for a long time. It provided Koreans with an escape from the rather stiff constraints of their hierarchical Confucian culture. In the eighteenth century, King Yongjo created fines for drinking alcohol intemperately, but the laws were flouted. The soju tents in Seoul were banned and frowned upon but still persist. The one real way to seal a friendship or business association is to drink together. That's why there are rituals surrounding drinking – as we have the round system in Anglo-Saxon culture. You don't drink with strangers, which is why I hadn't met people in bars in Seoul, I suspect. I realised that with Mr Che and Mr Kim on the beach at Pyonsan, with the staff from the Hard Rock Cafe and with my girlfriends in Kampo, I'd been sealing friendships by learning to drink with Koreans. Just as well, then, that I'd put my drinking boots on before I came to Korea.

Two hours passed and, though this had turned into a meal to remember, I was nervous about getting to Tanyang. I might not get another chance. 'Five more minutes,' said Wook, several times. When we eventually got up to pay, there was spilled booze on the table and the floor from over-zealous pouring.

'I think I have a *little* too much to drink,' slurred Wook, a touch glassy-eyed, as we left the restaurant, and he took my arm. I offered to carry his bag of vegetables for him, as he now pronounced them too heavy. 'I like you,' he began, 'because you are candid and direct, and…' He gave up and lapsed into prudent silence. Standing waiting to cross the road to go back to the bus station, he noticed for the first time my wooden bead bracelet.

'Are you Buddhist?' he asked.

'Well, no, it was a present from a friend,' I replied, thinking of Kim Cheung-suk in Kampo.

He nodded, and pointed to it again: 'This will guard you from difficult situations.'

Not all of them, I thought, smiling to myself.

At the station, Jae bought me a bag of sticky buns and announced he wanted me to accompany him and Wook back to Seoul. I reminded him yet again that I wanted to go to Tanyang, even though it was not the correct time of year to do so. Mayhem ensued, with Wook running back and forth to the ticket desk to prove that getting to Tanyang would be far too difficult, almost surely impossible. Grinning Jae had me rooted to the spot, and I wasn't arguing with an inebriated former *ssirum* wrestler, so before I knew it they had bought me a ticket to Seoul on the same bus as them. I relented. Perhaps they were right. It was funny to think of the early days in Seoul when I couldn't meet any Korean people. Now I couldn't seem to shake them off.

Before we boarded, I managed to buy a copy of the new *Korea Herald*. We got seats at the front of the bus, directly behind the driver. Wook sat next to me, while Jae, across the aisle, promptly fell asleep. As we set off, I opened the paper and found my Suwon article. Excited, I showed it to Wook, and he proceeded to read it out loud, very loudly in fact, until the driver barked at him to pipe down. Then Wook told me the piece was written at 'a rather low level' because I didn't know Korea very well, which wasn't the kind of reaction I was hoping for. He tried to wheedle back into my favour by asking carefully polite questions, and then making odd jokes about alliteration in the title, unaware he was breathing over me an overpowering combination of bean paste stew and soju. I couldn't help laughing.

Gradually he fell asleep. His head kept falling onto my shoulder, and in the interests of propriety I thought I'd offer him my inflatable travel pillow instead. He thanked me but explained it was unnecessary: he had a friend to lean on. I really had found a friend this time.

CHAPTER NINETEEN:

THE LAST DAYS OF SEOUL

About a quarter of Koreans are Christians. Christianity entered Korea through Jesuits from the Chinese imperial court in the eighteenth century, and spread quickly but was suppressed by the royal family. Those suspected of sympathising with Catholicism were violently repressed, tortured, even executed – just as the Shilla Dynasty had beheaded the first Buddhist monk to arrive, before deciding Buddhism wasn't such a bad idea after all. Christianity showed up again with American Protestant missionaries who founded schools and hospitals; and after the Korean War missionaries from Ireland came too.

On the way back from Puan, I had noticed a traditional ancestral burial mound on a hillside, with a statue of the Virgin Mary, which I'd thought a strange combination, but in fact Catholic and Protestant denominations thrive alongside Buddhism and Shamanism, and of course Confucianism, which is not quite a religion but certainly a moral framework.

After my telephone conversation with Immigration, I was dreading the trip there to extend my visa, not even knowing how I'd find it with those vague directions, 'get out at exit six and walk for ten minutes'. I took the subway out to Omokkyo, and got out at exit six. It was pouring with rain and had been raining hard, non-stop, for two days now. This really was monsoon, and it's no wonder Korea is such a green country. I tried to get directions from the few people out on the street in this atrocious weather. Gradually, it dawned on me. You're supposed to keep walking straight in the direction you're facing as you come up the steps of the exit. I supposed there was an ordered logic to it. It was funny how even at frenzied times of day, people kept to the correct side when going up or down the steps to the underground passages you needed to cross the busy roads.

I found Immigration and arrived just as most of the staff left for an hour's lunch break. I waited for an hour or so in my drenched shoes and clothes.

I passed time reading the signs on the walls. One said that the Nationality Law was amended in 1998, so that dual nationals who did not choose to become Korean would lose their Korean citizenship as of 14 June 2000. Interesting that you couldn't have dual nationality, you had to choose to be Korean or not. I also noticed a counselling room 'for non-Koreans who may be suffering unfair treatment or infringement of human rights by employers'. I'd heard that sometimes the schools treated foreign English teachers badly and refused to pay their wages, which seemed bizarre given the paramount importance given to education in this country. What did that say about the attitude to foreigners?

Finally, my number was called. The man at the desk was very confused that I didn't have an airline ticket to depart the country. I didn't buy a return ticket as I didn't know when I'd be returning home, or where from. Gav and I planned to cross the country to Pusan, the south-eastern tip of South Korea, and take a ferry to Japan for a week – I would automatically be granted another three months' visitor's visa when I returned, and then we could spend time travelling around Korea together before heading to China. So I just needed to extend my visa for this last week. Instead of having my itinerary documented in tickets, I wanted to go to Pusan and buy a ticket for the ship to Japan when I got there. This seemed to amuse the immigration officer – although I now realised that sometimes smiling was a sign of embarrassment in Korea. He couldn't believe I'd practically allowed my visa to expire, leaving only one day to renew it! I wasn't sure myself how it happened, and to Koreans, such lack of planning, such disregard for the rules and formalities, was unheard of. He was surprisingly nice and helpful, however, forgiving everything because I was a foreigner who was clearly mad. He made me write out an explanation of my situation on a piece of paper which he attached to the form, then told me that the application for an extension would be processed.

On the way back, as the train crossed the Han River, I saw the construction site of the new World Cup stadium, Mapogu Songam, which would be the biggest soccer stadium in Asia, holding 63,930 fans. Although they could have merely revamped the Olympic Stadium, they decided to build something new and symbolic, something strongly Korean. Apparently the design incorporated three themes: the octagonal shape was that of a traditional tray, the 'floating' roof was taken from the design of a kite, and the roof supports emulated a traditional Han River ship. Perhaps this would help them beat Japan. South Korea would host thirty-two World Cup matches in Seoul, Suwon, Inchon, Taegu, Pusan and other cities across the country, while the rest of the matches would happen in Japan.

Gav's contract had almost ended and suddenly we would have time together, evenings together. It would be interesting to see how things worked out. I had needed the times on my own, but was happy to be with my man again. I felt refreshed and fit from all my time in mountains and open air. Gav was fit too, from drumming almost every night for more than three months. We made plans to leave the day after his last show. Trying to plan the trip in an organised manner, I gathered all sorts of information on trains from the government English information service, probably a waste of time as the information always seemed to be wrong. I wondered if they didn't update it frequently enough, or if the English hadn't been checked properly for errors. There probably weren't enough people using it to make it worthwhile.

One evening, I finally visited Chongdong Theatre in central Seoul. Its show of traditional Korean dance and music was for tourists, but the performances were mesmerising. There was *samdopungmulgut*, five men playing powerful rhythms with gongs and drums, and *pangut*, a group of drummers who dance with trailing long white ribbons, full of raw, primal energy. Afterwards I walked through the city, passing through Namdaemun Market where I bought a beautiful celadon vase – the porcelain covered with a cracked, pale, cloudy blue-green glaze that is a prized Korean tradition – as a gift for my mother, though I wasn't quite sure how I'd get it home. The vase was simple, restrained, graceful, the qualities prized in Korea.

There was a phone call. 'It is Mr Kim. Can you remember me?' Mr Kim, hmm, might have to narrow it down a tad. But of course I did recognise his voice. It was Wook. He'd been in Soraksan with his family and unable to call earlier, but promised to pass on my best wishes to Jae, and to keep in touch by email. Meeting Mr Kim had been the culmination of a wonderful period of getting to know Korea, of learning that South Korea really was a place where you could come for happy memories, in spite of its centuries of troubles, particularly the last one.

We said goodbye to the Kimbap Ladies, and had a farewell lunch of *mandu ramyun*, noodles with dumplings, and kimchi. For the last show at the Hyatt, we bought bottles of beer at the supermarket and sneaked them backstage. One of the band's fans, a Swiss businessman called André, was there and so I had someone to dance with. During 'Hotel

California', Leroy unbelievably forgot the words and had to hum an entire verse, which didn't really work with that song. But nobody in the crowd seemed to notice apart from me, and the crowd demanded a couple of encores before Good Vibes finished its final show. Gav and I joined the others to celebrate at King Club in Itaewon.

It was a funny place, King Club: seedy, full of Russian prostitutes, and yet it looked like a bingo hall, set out with formica tables, and the waitresses were solid Korean women of a certain age, wearing the kind of uniforms you find in American diners. Dean was sitting with his arms round a homely waitress, presumably to hold himself up; he kept throwing cigarettes in the air to catch them in his mouth, but dropped most on the floor. Another waitress flashed her knickers at Vinny, but he was too glazed over with booze to notice. Moodily, Vinny and Dean both gave Gav unbridled grief for leaving the band, putting paid to Gav's hope that everything could end on a friendly note. Barry sat drinking shots with a thin Russian girl of about twenty who seemed to have her kid brother in tow. It was altogether a bizarre scene. Same as it ever was.

After, Gav and I went for one last Hyatt breakfast. Sweaty, laughing, probably still drunk in our dancing clothes, we swept past the immaculate staff and took our breakfast outside onto the balcony to escape the freezing air conditioning, and sat watching the grey city awakening.

Leaving music equipment and my rash pottery purchase in storage at the Hyatt, that night we caught the overnight train to Pusan.

PART THREE: WE'LL ALWAYS HAVE SEOUL

'The two days which you and Jae and I spent last summer will be remembered forever between ourselves. Hope to have cheerful days.'

Wook in Seoul

'Life demands that we offer something more – spirit, soul, intelligence, good–will…'

Henry Miller, *The Colossus of Maroussi*

CHAPTER TWENTY:

SLICED LAW FISH

English teachers in Korea often went to Japan on the overnight ferry to get a taste of luxury and comfort and western things you couldn't get in Korea. But in Japan something called 'Korea-envy syndrome' was emerging. A Japanese man had even started a blog about it. He'd discovered that Korean people were expressive and confident. He loved the busy markets, the passion and kindness, the music and movies. The country that had once brought Buddhism and temples to Japan was leading the way once more, this time with technology, ubiquitous high-speed broadband, home appliances that could be controlled across the net. Having embraced the Internet with creativity (online auctions, stock trading, game software industries), Korea was surpassing its powerful neighbour, which had been far slower to change.

Still, we were ready for a holiday in Japan. Crossing on the ferry from Pusan to Shimonoseki, we took a super-efficient train north to beautiful Kyoto, where the streets were calm and quiet, and there were grand and famous temples. At the glittering Temple of the Golden Pavilion, which Gav had longed to see after reading the Japanese author Yukio Mishima, everything was so manicured someone was actually sweeping fallen leaves off moss to keep it perfect. We walked together through palaces, took delight in open-air art galleries and funky shops with unfathomable names like 'Elephant – U Represent Individuality'. We ate sushi presented the same way as back home, in colourful packages, and delicous patisserie cakes. Gav bought a full-size replica samurai sword. He liked playing with it so much that, after I found myself cowering in the corner one night, I forbade him from taking it out of its box in our tiny hostel room after he'd had more than one drink. It was good to see him with energy again, no longer saying daily, 'I wish I didn't have to work tonight.'

The hostel had a social lounge where you could meet other travellers, and the porn videos and circular waterbeds so prevalent in Korean *yogwan* were conspicuously absent here. In a lively little neighbourhood bar we ate *yaki soba* fresh off the griddle and were welcomed cheerfully night after night. The woman thought Gav looked like a movie star and slapped him on the back shouting out the name of the stars she thought he resembled – 'Kevin Koss-ana!',

'Shan Connari!' One day we went for a long walk in the hills, and were thrilled to be caught in a rainstorm in the middle of a forest. We dried off in the sunshine, walking through immaculately designed gardens.

In Nara, a short journey from Kyoto, where deer roamed the streets, we visited more grand temples and pagodas, gorged ourselves at an all-you-can-eat sushi buffet, and bought cold Sapporo beer from vending machines on street corners. Then we took the sleek bullet train to Hiroshima, and spent reflective moments at the terrible spot that marks Ground Zero for the atomic bomb. Enquiring at the tourist office about cheap accommodation, we were asked, 'Would a campsite on an island do?' We set up our tent among the trees on an empty beach a short walk from the picturesque ancient temple of Miyajima, overlooking glittering blue waters. The days were hot and sunny but not stickily humid, so we could dress up like proper tourists, I in my short flowery dress, Gav in his yellow shirt and chinos. There was so much to do during those sunny days in Japan, and it was wonderful to be strolling around together with no stress, no rushing back for work.

Japan was sophisticated and lovely. The people were polite and helpful. And yet, after a while, perhaps we missed the madness of Korea, the effusiveness of the people, the unfathomable differences, the rough-around-edges quality. Besides, without doing anything extravagant, merely being in Japan was astonishingly expensive, twice as expensive as Korea. Even a segregated dorm bed in a stifling hot room with a curfew in Nara had cost far more than those sleazy but comfortable *yogwan* rooms in Korea. It was so tempting to eat sushi forever, but we had to leave before we ran out of money.

On the overnight ferry from Shimonoseki, we met a very large Japanese man in a white suit and a black waistcoat, with square black sunglasses. We encountered him in the snack bar in the evening where he insisted on buying fruit and ice cream, and sharing his beers with us. We bought him one in return, but he said it was dangerous to drink with him: 'I am a heavy drinker.' He had a business with a hundred employees in some kind of care for the elderly, he said. After we tried to buy him another beer, he told us, 'Don't worry, I am rich' — at which point he opened one of the pockets of his waistcoat and flashed a thick wad of 1,000-yen notes, thousands of dollars in cash.

At Customs and Immigration, re-entering Korea, we stood in orderly fashion behind the white line, waiting to be called. Suddenly, a crowd of middle-aged Koreans surged forward, pushing and shoving. Welcome to Korea. Eventually emerging into Pusan early in the morning, we were almost run over by an impatient motorbike trying to share the pavement. Welcome back to exasperating, inimitable Korea.

Pusan is Korea's biggest port on the Pacific, less than a day from the Russian port of Vladivostok, and just north of the East China Sea. The dockyards harboured hundreds of big sea-going ships. You could board one of these ships and cross the world. It was a big, hectic, confusing port city, industrial and industrious, the streets full of dust and noise and chaos. Yet behind the white high-rise buildings, the typical Korean green, forested hills rose up into gentle peaks.

The humid, monsoonal summer had given way to clear blue autumnal skies, cool sunny days. The fish market was full of cheery women squatting on the ground shucking huge clams and oysters and mussels. The seafood here glistened on ice, as in every country market I'd seen in Korea but bigger and fresher: purpleish squid with staring eyes, sleek silver-grey fish, rock-like shells as big as your fist. Mosquito coils kept flies at bay, leaving an incense aroma in the air on top of the strong briny smell that was like a mouthful of ocean. Strong women with fast knives and gold-toothed smiles sat emptying shells into heaping tureens.

It was surely time to try the Korean *fweh*, raw fish, or 'sliced law fish' as they'd called it in Inchon. There had always been reasons not to try it before. One was the expense, because the cheapest plate was 20,000 won, the same price as a room for the night. Also because of those weird sea creatures writhing in tanks outside the *fweh* restaurants, huge squid and various mollusks, including that red thing that resembled nothing more than a human heart. How would you know what to order? People happily sat at market stalls munching away beside tanks of writhing eels and fat brown sea slugs. In three months of attempting to cross this cultural Pacific, I was barely treading water. The progress I'd made was feeble, such as eating dried squid instead of peanuts with beer.

We screwed down our courage at the 'Beer Mart', a hideously decorated upstairs bar with no atmosphere whatsoever – we were back in Korea, no doubt about that. Then we returned to the fish market, prowling past outdoor stalls covered in orange tarpaulins, where couples were eating slowly with chopsticks. Unfortunately, there were no menus, and none of the dishes bore any resemblance to anything we'd eaten before.

At last, we stopped beside a busy, lively restaurant that opened onto the street, where stews bubbled away on stoves set in the middle of each table. Two diners beckoned us to take the only empty table, giving their food two thumbs-up. So we sat and placed our order by pointing at what they were eating, a stew in red sauce, cooked in tin foil and eaten with lettuce, garlic and bean paste. This could be good.

Our food arrived minutes later, and whatever it was, it was still moving. Our dinner was pink and squirming. I tried not to look too closely, but out of the corner of my eye it seemed like those little wriggling eels I'd often seen leaping about in plastic tubs in the market – except now they had apparently been chopped up into pieces and skinned and were writhing about.

'They're not really alive,' Gav said. 'It's just electrical impulses.'

'Just like sashimi really, only fresher,' I replied, turning green. We tried to talk across the table without looking down at the awkwardly alive-looking things trying to get our attention as they cooked in the middle of the table.

'You can't get fish fresher than this.'

'A real cultural experience.'

'I just wish they'd stop moving.'

'Me too.'

We looked at the pictures on the walls, at all the other people happily eating. For a moment, the food seemed to stop moving, but the *ajumma* came by and turned up the heat, which started it jumping again.

Eventually she came back when it stopped moving again, and said the food was ready to eat, which is what we were afraid of. We asked for more hot pepper sauce. And bravely we started eating. It didn't taste great.

Two young guys at the next table were gorging on some delicious-looking shellfish stew, and we eyed it jealously. They sent over a bowl of it for us, and then a couple of glasses of soju. We'd never been so grateful for that toxic-smelling inebriant, and shouted a thankful *kombae*, cheers, as we downed the shots.

Feeling somewhat nauseous, still not quite sure how we managed to eat whatever it was, we paid and said our thank yous, and got away from the scene of the crime. We wandered further into the market, which was now lit up by strings of light bulbs as people strolled the gleaming alleys and shopped. We found ourselves entering a huge hall, bright with electric lights hanging over fish tanks. Huge tanks were everywhere, rows and rows of them at individual stalls, where people sat at tables and big pipes hung down to keep the water fresh. We walked around taking photos, dodging busy stallholders in their rubber boots and full-length rubber aprons and gloves.

One stallholder who spoke English approached us and we asked out of curiosity how much a raw fish cost. It was expensive, 30,000 won (US$30), as you had to buy the whole fish. But he was happy for us simply to look at the weird creatures in his tanks. I burst out laughing when I saw creatures that looked like smooth pink penises, changing shape as they took in water at one end and expelled it again at the other. The guy picked one out and squeezed til it sprayed a thin stream across the stall to general hysteria, and he whispered something to Gav, with a universal gesture suggesting virility. Gav said he was OK in that department, thanks.

It was rowdy, noisy, the place to be in Pusan. As we walked around, a group of people I'd caught in one of my photos beckoned me over. They asked me to sit down with them in the insistent manner of those who've had a fair bit to drink and won't take no for an answer. The table was covered with green bottles and plates of fish. When Gav found me again, I was doing a shot of soju with my new friends. They were young office workers, the men in short-sleeved checked shirts and the woman in geeky specs and a bob haircut, and they all handed us their business cards to show they worked for an ISM management company. There was much shouting of *kombae* and much demanding of 'One shot!' and much taking of photos, much smoking and shouting, much slurring of words and dropping things. I had visions of my camera going in the fish tank. But I finally got to taste some Korean sashimi, some *fweh*. It was thin slices of a white fish, clean-tasting, beautiful.

When we found an opportunity to leave, and perhaps save ourselves from a monumental soju hangover, the woman of the group, Miss Choi, came along to show us the way, and dragged us by the arm, insisting on taking us to the nearest hotel, despite our protestations that we already had a place to stay.

'I am sorry,' she said, 'my English is not very good,' and she dragged us on. We couldn't quite find a way to make her understand or politely shake her off. Then as we waited to cross the road, another man said hello and proceeded to paw Gav's arm hair, feeling his biceps, not letting go until I removed the probing hand myself. We finally reached the un-needed hotel and said goodnight to the persistent Miss Choi and the pawing stranger, and burst out laughing.

CHAPTER TWENTY-ONE:

HAPPY AS A SQUID IN SOUP

In the morning, we reluctantly left our comfortable room in Pusan. We had a couple of bottles of beer left over, so we gave them away to a baffled man on the street. Unfortunately, the good karma didn't take immediate effect. We sat down in a cafe and were asked to leave because we had backpacks. So instead we caught a bus to Tongdo. We'd see the temple there, and continue up the east coast to Soraksan.

We had been tempted to travel south to Chejudo, the large semitropical island renowned for its beauty, its dormant volcano, yellow mustard flowers, Easter Island-like grandfather statues, and women who dive for sea urchins. But it was a holiday resort, a popular honeymoon destination. A 'must-see' place, we feared it could be costly and commercialised, full of photo opportunities. We'd explore the east coast instead. After all, I'd had some of my best adventures when simply wandering through the less famous places. I wanted Gav to experience the same magic.

From the windows of a school in Tongdo, kids hung out of the windows shouting, 'Where are you from? Where are you going?' We smiled and waved, then made our way towards the temple entrance, playing Botticelli, a way of passing the time while travelling together. Gav was irritatingly good at the game. In *The Young Ones*, the TV comedy we'd bonded over, there's an episode in which Rick explains in painstaking fashion to Viv how to play Botticelli, otherwise known as 'Twenty Questions', using the astronaut Neil Armstrong as an example. On this particular occasion I managed to ask Gav twenty questions about who he was without guessing that he was in fact Neil Armstrong. It was most annoying. Whenever it was my turn, Gav guessed almost immediately.

A friendly man let us put our backpacks in his shed at the temple entrance, and we had a pleasant walk under big trees beside a wide stream gushing over boulders, Buddhist inscriptions carved into the rocks along the way. Halfway to the temple was a museum with a famous collection of Buddhist paintings, only open a few hours a day because of the delicate nature of the eighteenth-century paintings in ground minerals on silk. Though it was well after the specified closing time, the curator unlocked the door for us and let us in. They were huge paintings, depicting how all life is suffering, while high above the Buddha sat serenely detached from it all.

Tongdosa, an important Buddhist temple, was peaceful. Clouds obscured the mountain, said to resemble the mountain in India where Buddha delivered many sermons. The temple was founded here during the reign of the Shilla queen Sondok – the same time as Kirimsa. Korean monks traditionally took ordination at the so-called 'Diamond Platform', a special, decorative (but not diamond-encrusted) enclosure supposed to enshrine relics of Buddha. The wooden buildings had dragon carvings in the buttresses, elaborately painted exterior walls and ceilings and beams. Yet the halls were simple and bare except for an altar, a small table holding a book, clock, bell and gong, and a satin cushion for kneeling. After the gold and imperial pomp of Japanese temples, Tongdosa seemed humble, peaceful. I bowed to a monk, hoping we might be invited to talk to him, but he just bowed back.

We returned to town and ended up eating overpriced pizza that tasted nothing at all like pizza in a chalet-style building with an alpine theme and a bullying waiter. The next day, we struggled up the east coast on buses that battled through traffic, stuck in eight lanes of standstill around Ulsan, and were subjected to utter confusion and loud buzzers at Pohang station; until finally we found ourselves on the picturesque coast road to Samchok, with waves crashing up on a rocky shore to the right, and mountains to the left. At a rest stop, we got out of the bus to feel salt spray in a freezing wind. The temperatures were rapidly cooling now that it was September. It went dark after seven and the reading lights on the bus didn't work.

A cab at Samchok bus station agreed to take us to Samchok beach. There was drizzling rain and a cold wind as we searched for a place to stay, and nothing seemed open. I felt like crying. Finally, a woman came out of a restaurant and guided us into a plush, new building, showing us a brand-new, spotless room. She even agreed to rent it for a price we could afford. We bought pots of instant noodles and sat on a bed of quilts, watching CNN, listening to the big waves crashing on the beach as we fell asleep.

The sky was pale grey when I woke but it was good to see the open horizon, so while Gav lay sleeping, I went for a walk on the beach. The pale yellow sand was covered in rubbish: bottle tops, empty cigarette packets, instant noodle cartons, all manner of plastic wrappers and polystyrene containers that might have washed into shore or been left there after the rubbish ladies had finished for the season. Then there were the buildings, a row of new office-type buildings with odd misfit features in primary colours and mirrored glass. So much for the Korean desire to live in harmony with nature. At either end of the bay were military outposts, sentry boxes in camouflage colours, and razor-wire fences blocked off the cliffs. Samchok was in fact one of the first places to be attacked at the start of the Korean War.

When I got back to the room, Gav was watching more CNN. Then came the breakfast challenge. The only restaurant served whole raw fish only, even though the owners were eating a slap-up meal of rice and vegetables which looked tantalisingly good. They directed us to a cafe, which refused to serve us at all. We jumped into a cab to go back to the station, and the taxi driver tried to charge us for a detour to get some petrol. At the station we hoped to have some breakfast, but there was a bus going north ready to leave, and the information desk didn't understand my attempts to find out when the next bus after this one was leaving, so we hurried onto the bus.

Looking glumly out the window at dead trees, industrial landscapes and mangy cats, I wondered why everything was going wrong. Perhaps because I was no longer *honja*, no one seemed to care very much. Two people travelling together are left to themselves. Maybe if I were on my own I'd take more chances? I felt sad that Gav hadn't been able to sample the experiences or the spontaneous kindness I had found during the summer.

People could be mean-spirited, logistics could be difficult, anywhere in the world. Maybe people were sad the weather was turning cold. We were outsiders in a place unused to outsiders, and still only had a rudimentary grasp of the language. It was hardly surprising when plans didn't always go well. Discovering Korea, you never knew how things would turn out. I was lucky to have done so much. I tried to remind myself of Buddhist ways: you have to take the good with the bad, not cling to difficulties or despair but keep moving. *This time, once past, will never more return.* Perhaps it was time for us to move on.

The scenery improved as we continued north. The sun came out from behind the clouds, turning the sea deep blue, the waves trailing white spray, helping me ignore the barbed-wire fences and military outposts. At Naksan, we found a cosy little room above a fish restaurant for a tiny price, because it was out of season and there was no hot water. The sea was too cold for swimming, but we waded in up to our knees anyway.

Naksan was a pretty seaside town, but I never need to see as many dead squid again as I saw hanging to dry on its streets. Racks and racks of them, cleaned and splayed out, row upon row in their thousands. Everywhere I turned there was another rack of drying squid. Sadly, the Koreans are guilty of using terrifyingly destructive driftnet vessels to harvest squid from the depths of the Pacific Ocean. They have a large appetite for squid. I surveyed this bizarre scene of maritime massacre and thought of the cartoon smiling squid on packets of dried *ochinga* or *ochinga*-flavoured noodles: happy as a squid in soup.

As dusk fell, flashing neon signs were lighting up the night sky declaring discos and fun, but Naksan by night was chilly and deserted. Afer a delicious *dolsot bibimbap*, the kind served in a hot earthenware bowl that continues cooking as you eat it, and then a beer at a funereally quiet bar/coffee shop, we went to bed early out of boredom. We huddled under quilts on the floor, and cranked the under-floor *ondol* heating so high it kept blowing the fuse.

The most beautiful mountains on the Korean peninsula were said to be the Kumgang or Diamond Mountains, but since the war these had been inaccessible in North Korea.

Soraksan, or Snow Rock Mountain, was considered by many to be the most beautiful part of South Korea. It was in the very north-east, close to the thirty-eighth parallel, and many North Koreans were thought to have escaped and settled there. With its jagged rock spires, Soraksan was so popular with hikers and rockclimbers that the trails had to be closed for 'sabbatical years' from time to time. Its peaks were full of waterfalls named after dragons, ancient Buddhist hermitages and steep, rugged cliffs; the park had a wealth of animal species including the endangered grey bear, and plants including junipers and edelweiss.

Soraksan was ranked – in a country that loved to rank everything – as one of the top three mountains in the country, along with Chirisan in the south, and volcanic Hallasan on the island of Cheju; the highest peak of each rose over a mile above sea level. So although mountains covered seventy per cent of Korea's land area, making it one of the most mountainous regions in the world, going to Soraksan was seen as somehow better than going to less famous mountains. It was the ultimate 'must-see' in a 'must-see' culture. There were many famous things to see there, too: famous rocks, hiking routes, and the 'eight wonders', which included summer thunderstorms, moving rocks and caves. There were also 'eight views', corresponding to different seasons: the scent of spring, spring flowers, ascending dragons (waterfalls), rainbows, the sea of fog in summer, autumn foliage, moonlit peaks when the full moon rose high in the autumn sky and the rocks looked like 'dancing nymphs', and snow patterns on trees and rocks.

In spite of my misgivings about this sort of sightseeing, like the 'museum without walls' in Kyungju, we just couldn't leave Korea without seeing Soraksan. The Korean people would be very disappointed. This was my final concession to travelling the Korean way, my final gesture of accommodation to Korean culture. And in spite of the emptiness of Naksan the previous night, we appeared to have picked a national holiday to visit. The entrance was swarming with hordes of people. We set off up the mountain alongside them to experience Soraksan the true Korean way.

Somehow, in the midst of all this, the huge Buddha at the first temple towering above the crowds conjured calm and gentleness in the mere curve of its fingers. Pilgrims were bowing, kneeling, laying their head and hands on the ground in prayer. I remembered the photos Cheung-suk gave me of herself and her husband here.

Next stop on the route was the Moving Rock or Rocking Rock, a big boulder which supposedly could be shifted by the touch of your finger. It was not enough to see something famous, however: you had to have your photograph taken in front of it, which is why some fifty people were queueing to get to it. I went one better and had Gav take my photo in front of the queue of people waiting to have their photo taken in front of the Rocking Rock.

The path to Ulsanbawi Peak continued uphill pretty steeply, although as usual lithe Korean women in tight jeans and high-heeled sandals were tripping up it like mountain goats without breaking a sweat. Serious hikers wore colourful socks pulled up to their knees and the full sporty regalia. We stopped with other crowds at a rest area with food and drinks and souvenirs, and discovered we were about three quarters of the way there already. Energetically, we resumed our pace, and then suddenly we saw a huge, sheer rock face ahead, rising up like some awful dragon's tooth, and a tiny steel staircase clinging to it. That was the last quarter of the way to Ulsanbawi.

There was a spirit of camaraderie as we all marched up to the start of the steel staircase. How did they build it? Could it take everyone's weight? We took it one step at a time, step, step, step, all the way up, legs aching, not wanting to complain as there were others carrying children on their shoulders.

And finally we were at the top, looking out across the bare peaks that gave way to green forest sweeping down to the valleys. Sheer rock steeples reached finger-like into the sky around us. The only sound was the wind that blew clouds of mist across the cliffs, covering then revealing the scenes below. According to legend, Ulsanbawi was too late to make it to Kumgang where all the most beautiful rocks were, so it stayed here instead for the nice scenery. The only disappointment was that the stall selling 'I Climbed Ulsanbawi' badges was closed.

By the time we returned to the temple below, a bright, almost full moon shone over the darkened statue of Buddha in a dark grey sky. It was cold. The leaves had started changing colour, and in a few months there would be snow here. Rivers would freeze over. It was hard to imagine after the heat and rain and sunshine of summer. I thought of the monks in their isolated hermitages in the mountains, white with snow and ice.

A slow boat to Shanghai would leave in a couple of days, and we planned to be on it. So the next morning, after an icy shower, we had to take the bus to Kangnung. This wasn't easy, as it was apparently pronounced something like Kangreung, and I couldn't get anyone to understand. Then in Kangnung, we needed to find a bank to get money for our bus tickets back to Seoul. However, the bank machine in the station didn't work – and on asking directions at the Tourist Information Centre to the biggest bank, I discovered that all the banks were closed for the public holiday.

I pleaded with the young woman in the Tourist Information Centre to change US\$20 to won so we could make our connection to Seoul. These slow boats to Shanghai didn't run very often. She giggled at my admittedly ridiculous suggestion, and said it was impossible because she didn't know the exchange rate. Not to be deterred, I asked her to look it up on the Internet, and she thought that was a reasonable proposal, and changed some money for me.

On the bus we sat in a traffic jam for hours, but finally made it to Seoul and our connection to Inchon, from where we would take our ship. I rang the shipping company number again to confirm, and was told we didn't have tickets reserved after all, even though they'd been booked a week earlier by the Tourist Information Centre in Pusan. We made our way to the shipping company's offices anyway, where a guard told us there were absolutely no ships to Shanghai. Could we just go in and talk to the people in the office anyway, I asked?

Inside a dark warehouse there was a cabin, where they said there was a ship to Shanghai and that we did have tickets booked on it, but that the crossing would take slightly longer than the usual crossing because of a typhoon.

It wasn't easy leaving Korea.

With the excitement of the travels ahead, I didn't dwell too much on saying goodbye. Something had been telling me it was time to go. I had my happy memories and my stories to take away, and Wook would be keeping in touch. The typhoon turned into a super-tornado, leaving the ship anchored just outside Inchon harbour for a couple of days. Held in limbo, I reflected on my Korean summer.

CHAPTER TWENTY-TWO:

COMFORT ME WITH KIMCHI

Two days ago I met Jae in Seoul and enjoyed talking about you and your pictures… The two days which you and Jae and I spent will be remembered forever between ourselves. If you come to Korea again, I and Jae would be happy and prepare everything more systematically. Hope to have cheerful days. I wait for your frequent mail.

Bye-bye (annyung).

Wook in Seoul.

Our extra-slow boat made it to Shanghai, and we crossed China to within a stone's throw of Tibet; then went south to Thailand and a perfect tropical beach for the final two weeks before the flights back home. On the Khao San Road in Bangkok, we found a Korean restaurant, and ate there twice on our last day. Somehow, we made it through one of the weirdest, most challenging starts to a relationship you could have, and we kept wearing those silver rings we'd bought in Itaewon. We'd always have Seoul.

Back in Toronto, we devoured cheese sandwiches and microbrewery beer with gusto, while trying to figure out what this 'real life' was that everyone kept saying we had to adjust back to. Rooms felt very cluttered with unnecessary furniture, as we were used to sitting on the floor; the apartment seemed outlandishly large. In spite of being somewhat disoriented, I felt a sense of possibility. When Gav went back into the Irish pub where he had worked before – so long ago, it seemed now – one of the waitresses propping up the bar in her usual spot said, 'Hey, didn't you go away somewhere?' before turning back to her gossip. For them, half a year had disappeared in routine, while we would never be the same people again.

I worked from home and would make a bastardised *bibimbap* for lunch some days, steaming the rice while I chopped vegetables, fried an egg, added red pepper paste. When I craved comfort food, I'd head to Little Korea for a bubbling hot *kimchi tchigae*. The man in the Korean-run convenience store where I bought the square plastic packages of kimchi-flavoured *shin ramyun* always asked, 'You can eat?' and, fanning his mouth, 'Very spicy!' Coming home late at night, I gorged on kimchi straight from the tub with my chopsticks, which I'm sure any

Korean would say is simply not done. My home-rolled *kimbap* never came out very well, although I'd bought the proper rolling mat in Seoul. But I could fold a square of salted dried seaweed around a mouthful of sticky rice using steel chopsticks. And I would always eat my *bibimbap* with a spoon.

I kept in touch with Wook by email, and told him about the problems of adjusting to life back home.

Glad to hear about your latest life. The reason why settling back is hard, I think, that you have made too long a journey. Everyone tends to feel unsettled and solitary after a travelling through many strange foreign lands. I hope everything will be OK with you. Your last two meals with Gavin in Bangkok, especially having *bibimbap* and *kimchi tchigae*, was touching and impressive even to me. I think you can get over the icy cold wilds of Toronto by always thinking of the warm sunshine and waters of Hwayangdong Valley in Korea. My life here is always regular and interesting – weekends in mountains or seasides and the rest of a week in Seoul.

I asked him a Korean language question, and I almost wished I hadn't. I wanted to check that the phrase *Odi gan* I'd heard in Korea did indeed mean 'Where are you going?' He replied that this was incomplete 'and a little mistaken', that 'Where are you going?' was *Dangsin odiro gal gutsinga*. Another email followed the same day, expanding on the point.

I'll explain it in detail – the sentence 'Where are you going?' in English has two meanings: when it is future form, it means

'Where will you go?' and when it is progressive form, it means 'Now where are you going for?' In case of the former, 'Where will you go?' is read as 'Dangsin Odiro Gal Gutsinga?' in Korea. In case of progressive form, it is read as 'Dangsin Odiro Ga Go itsum niga?' in Korea.

Good Luck to you. Addio (=An nyung=Bye-bye)
Wook-hyuon

I wrote back to him again, confused and puzzled, because '*Odi gan?*' was a question I'd heard and responded to several times, and I was sure I couldn't be that mistaken. I'd only written to him to check the spelling, really. He wrote back, now confusing me even further by telling me that my understanding of *odi gan* was 'absolutely correct and precise'. Sigh. I wasn't going to master the Korean language anytime soon.

Glad to receive your mail again. It is a little getting colder and colder in Seoul. The weather at Naksan in September was freakly cold. But now Naksan is very cold, maybe below zero. GOOD LUCK to you. I hope to have frequent connection with you.

An nyung (=Bye)
WOOK-hyuon'

I was moved by his warm, unreserved friendship. He hardly knew me, and yet he would offer his help and hospitality, as so many other Koreans had done during my summer there. This is not something you find everywhere in the world. The American Henry Miller described his friendships with

Greeks in 1939 that way in *The Colossus of Maroussi*. Long may such friendship continue.

My summer in Korea happened at a historic time, with the peace summit between North and South, Chairman Kim meeting President Kim. The sunshine policy of South Korean President Kim Dae-jung earned him the Nobel Peace Prize, and it made South Koreans more eager for reunification.

Riots continued: in October 2000 they were against globalisation and free market policies; in March 2001 riot police broke up a strike at the Daewoo factory over job cuts. But South Korea's economy was flourishing again, with the occasional trade spat with China over export tariffs on Korean cellular phones and cheap Chinese garlic.

South Korea continued to prepare for the World Cup, completed the new Seoul Stadium for less money than it cost the British Football Association merely to buy the Wembley site in London, and created a nifty bit of urban renewal too. A municipal rubbish dump near the stadium was sealed and then grassed over to create a golf course and ecology park overlooking the river, while pipes inserted into the former tip would carry gas to a newly built village to fuel it for sixteen years. In 2002, not only did South Korea host the World Cup with aplomb, in ten superb stadiums, but – famously – its team beat Italy. The stands were a blur of red as the Korean fans rose up as one and went bananas. Imagine the soju consumed that night.

My dad, who writes about football and was there when Korea got knocked out of the World Cup in the semifinals, says that when Germany scored a winning goal against them, the cheering in the stands went deathly quiet for a moment; and then it simply continued as before, as happily as ever.

Unfortunately, while Korean people are hospitable, warm and good-humoured, most foreigners tend to encounter the stony face of Seoul. It's not very welcoming being laughed at in restaurants or told to leave, not easy getting around when taxi drivers are short tempered. Yet it makes your day when a complete stranger comes up to you in the street and asks if they can help you. And on getting out of Seoul, you begin to understand why Koreans are so proud of their country.

Korean culture must be one of the least diluted in the world, especially for such an advanced nation. This is beginning to change in a tiny way. Because the male population is bigger than the female and women are becoming more successful and financially independent, South Korean men are actually looking elsewhere in Asia for wives. But for some time after the Korean War, a mixed-race child born of an American father and Korean mother could be stoned as a non-person, as Elizabeth Kim recounts so poignantly in her memoir *Ten Thousand Sorrows*. She says 'the intense love for the country's heritage and traditions has its darker side of hatred for anything that taints the purity of that heritage'.

Korean nationalism has for centuries been a weapon to protect their freedom and independence from foreign aggression, or to preserve Korean identity in times of foreign invasion. It is a powerful force, although it must have broken down at some point on the road that led to Korea being divided. Yet the Korean people have never sought domination over another nation. Perhaps it's because there is spirituality at the heart of the culture: Seon masters who live in simple poverty, meditating in silence, living in harmony with nature. While Koreans strive for economic growth, they have a place in their hearts for the simple life away from the city and material things. They're also a people who have massacred and repressed their own, who litter their beaches and build ugly buildings, of course. It's hard to generalise.

Pride in the Korean way has kept traditions alive. As a foreigner, you learn the Korean way, or you stay within the foreigner zones, the Special Tourism Zones.

Wilfred Thesiger, the British explorer of Arabia, believed that our ability to travel easily 'has shrunk the world, and robbed it of its diversity'. I don't think it has, thankfully. In spite of half a century of American influence, South Korea has adopted only those things it found useful – perhaps the middle-class American dream – and made them Korean, but it doesn't want to be anything other than Korean. That's just as well. There are few enough places that remain enigmatic to westerners.

South Korea's pop culture has been spreading through Asia since 2000 in what is called the Korean Wave or Hallyu. Across Asia, audiences are enthralled by the storylines, intimate relationships, outstanding technical quality and good-looking stars of Korean soap opera. Korean success on large and small screens has led to a big new investment project: Hallyu-wood. China is beginning to envy South Korea not only for its pop stars but for the marriage of individual happiness and sophisticated consumerism with Confucian values about family loyalty, something China lost during the Cultural Revolution. South Korea has modernised and yet retained its traditions.

The spirit of Korea is forward-thinking yet ancient too, on the cutting edge of technology but clinging proudly to its soju tents and shamanism; reserved and serious in the pursuit of education and wealth, yet enjoying life, laughing, singing on the top of a moutain; seeking to balance the individual needs with the community needs. As the nation gains stature, a more confident new South Korea is emerging, proud of its traditions but happy to welcome the world. I can only hope that this nation will never lose its freedom again.

The peace talks began to be overshadowed by the fear of a growing nuclear programme and unstable government in the North. North Korea is known to have the largest land army in the world, over a million soldiers increasingly deployed towards the border, according to Robert Kaplan in *Atlantic Monthly*; it has missiles trained on Seoul, so that nobody can invade North Korea without causing massive casualties in the South. It has stockpiles of biological and chemical weapons. US Vice President Dick Cheney was famously quoted as saying the only reason the United States invaded Iraq instead of a similarly rogue state like North Korea is that Iraq was 'do-able'. Robert Kaplan stated: 'Totalitarian regimes close to demise are apt to get panicky and do rash things. The weaker North Korea gets, the more dangerous it becomes.'

On the other hand, sudden reunification of the Korean peninsula could be devastating to the economy and society of South Korea. But since the reunions in 2000, more than 9,000 family members from North and South Korea have been temporarily reunited, with over 100,000 more applying to be considered.

Many things have changed since 2000. There is more and more exciting architecture, for example, and wine expert Jancis Robinson reported in 2007 that there now seemed to be more wine bars in Seoul than in London, with wine prices not much higher than the United Kingdom and United States. In fact, singer Kim Soo Hee on a visit to London in 2007 talked about a recipe for kimchi with wine taking Seoul by storm.

In early 2008, the fifteenth-century city gate of Namdaemun, which had survived Japanese invasions and the Korean War, burned down as a result of arson. Wook wrote:

'Here in Seoul most people are in awful sorrow and distress as if they lost their parents. But the past is only the past. Koreans will reconstruct the second Namdaemun as grandly as it used be.'

Annyung haseyo means go peacefully, go in peace. One of the gifts I took away from Korea was a greater awareness of Buddhist thinking – mindfulness, making a difference in everything we do. Bad things that happen in life have been caused by us – collectively. By each person striving to do what's best, all of us have better futures. Perhaps we have a responsibility to help South Korea remain the free country it is today, and to be aware of what is happening to those suffering under the regime in North Korea. Buddhism means a more philosophical life. The way to truth is within ourselves, and we should enjoy a worthwhile life as much as we can.

When I quit my job and went to South Korea, people said, 'You're so brave, I wish I could do that.' Well, why not? It simply means giving up some creature comforts for a while. If we can't learn to sleep on the floor and go without the things we depend on in everyday life, if we can't leave certain events to chance, what possibility is there for enlightenment, for real happiness? When caught in routine, we are seldom learning new ways to make the most of life. From time to time we must take a break to discover a new path and to open up the possibility of being surprised.

As with all long breaks from work, this time gave me the chance to reassess what I wanted out of life, what I was capable of. I had needed to be thrown into challenging, unfamiliar situations. Maybe I also needed to learn what a blessing it is to make friends, especially in other countries. The fact that people like Wook cared enough to keep in touch and offer me hospitality, for no other reason than friendship, is moving and gives hope.

I hope my time in Korea also taught me to be welcoming and hospitable to others when given the opportunity. When we really travel, we absorb part of the culture and take something away with us. I think of it as 'souvenirs': memories, intangible cultural properties. There were so many stories to tell of that summer, and I was anxious to preserve them, and eventually put them all together to try to thank the Korean people in the only way I could, by showing others it can be a place to go to acquire happy memories. I'd got the inspiration I needed – found it in every little town and village and temple I visited – although what I have written about Korea is at 'a rather low level', as Wook might say.

Today I'm in Woo Jung, one of my favourite Korean eateries in London, eating squid fried in sweet chilli sauce with crunchy vegetables, with rice and kimchi and cold barley tea. There are still so many dishes to try. The young couple sitting beside me order about half of the menu and sit concentrating on their food, although the guy talks on his mobile while picking dumplings out of his soup bowl. Even young Koreans take their food seriously. It's by no means an exclusively Korean crowd here, or at any of the other Korean restaurants I've started to frequent. *Annyung haseyo*, calls the waiter as more young people come in. I stop in to the Korean/Japanese supermarket across the street to buy kimchi, and then venture into the Seoul Bakery, where the friendly Korean lady urges me to try her different cakes, all baked on the premises, and I find pure heaven in the form of a warm eggy cake filled with walnuts, raisins, sesame seeds and honey.

Maybe it's strange for me to be so hooked on things Korean when I only spent three months there, it occurs to me. But then I meet an English man who runs an entire website dedicated to things Korean, even though his only link to Korea is that he had a Korean girlfriend once for a year and a half and likes Korean film. So perhaps it's not so unusual to be drawn to this exciting culture. Korea will always be a part of my life now, and it's appropriate that one element of that is food, since food is such an important part of Korean life. And food is something we can enjoy every day. Why not make a harmless ritual pleasure of it?

Gav hadn't really found his dream with the band in Korea, but he now only remembers the good times, and there are days when he dreams of going off to the other side of the world to play music. He reminisces about being 'a rock star in Asia', and when I laugh he reminds me, 'Hey, I signed autographs, man!' Good Vibes continued to get international gigs, and he almost went back to join them once. He joined another band for a while, but grew tired of the uncertainty of the music business and decided sensibly to hedge his bets and get a law degree. Gav and I moved to England together, and after our Korean adventure spent seven wonderful years together. We are still the best of friends.

After standing in King Muryong's tomb and walking in Korean hills, I was happy to be back in England and have history and nature close by. Britain has a Korean population of about 30,000, most living in London. Korean friends tell me that many come to England for the high level of education for their children, anxious to catch up on their education and skills after the devastating effects of the war. For ten years after the war there was no education, no teachers, and so the children of parents who grew up at that time also suffered.

When I started looking for Korean cafes in London, a favourite became the Bibimbab Cafe near the British Museum. One day, I was sitting in there with a cup of green tea and sheltering from a freak summer rainstorm. When the rain didn't stop, I bought another cup and lingered a little longer with my book. Eventually I thought I'd better just venture out anyway – but the kind Korean owner said I should stay to shelter there as long as I wanted, and even offered me a free cup of tea.

I'm happy that I explored Korea in my own way, not the systematic Korean way but blundering into strange situations and finding my own path. Wandering is good for surprises, and I still prefer unpredictable travel. As Wook said, we are unsettled by long travels, but to me that can be good. It's important to go your own way, to follow your instincts and be unsettled. Let a path lead you somewhere, and see where you end up.

KIMCHI RECIPE

Kimchi recipes vary a lot. Here is a simple one.

Ingredients:
2 kg Chinese cabbage
500 g salt
20 g coarse chilli flakes
20 g garlic
20 g spring onions
20 g ginger
10 ml Korean fish sauce
water

Remove a few outer leaves from the cabbage and set them aside. Cut the cabbage in half, cover it with salt or brine and leave overnight. Then rinse it well in fresh water.

Mix the chilli, garlic, onions, ginger and fish sauce with water to form a thick-ish paste or marinade. Spread the paste over each leaf of the cabbage, making sure it's completely covered. Wrap the whole thing in the outer leaves of the cabbage and leave in a jar to ferment in a cool place for up to a week, depending on how sour you like it.

Slice it into bite-sized pieces, about two inches square. Store in the fridge.

FURTHER INFORMATION ABOUT SOUTH KOREA

TEN THINGS TO DO

- Visit an ancient Buddhist monastery, preferably one that's not too famous.
- Hike in the mountains in one of the national parks.
- If you're there in May, witness the Confucian rites and music performed only once a year at Seoul's Chongmyo Shrine.
- Go to one of the many local festivals around the country, such as the mud or firefly festival.
- Camp on a beach and swim in the Yellow Sea.
- See a traditional drumming and dance performance.
- If you're there in winter, go skiing or to a hot springs resort.
- Experience real Korean nightlife by sharing dinner with locals and join them at a singing room.
- Spend the day or night exploring Namdaemun or Tongdaemun Market.
- Fly to the semitropical volcanic island of Chejudo.

TEN TRAVEL TIPS

- Learn how to say thank you = *kamsa hamnida* (usually shortened to *kamsamnida*) and please = *chuseyo*
- Take off your shoes whenever you enter homes, hotel rooms or certain restaurants and leave them with the other shoes near the door.

  Eat rice with a spoon, but use chopsticks for noodles and for picking food off the main and side dishes in the middle of the table. Hold chopsticks or spoon in your right hand. Never stick your chopsticks in the food, and especially not in the rice bowl (this is associated with death). Leave them resting on the table. Don't pick up food with your fingers.

  If you're eating spicy food you can wipe your nose but it's considered rude to blow your nose at the table.
- Not all ATMs accept foreign debit cards. They must say Global Service, so find a reliable one and use it – try a major hotel. You can get a cash advance on your credit card from a bank and most major hotels, restaurants and shops will accept credit cards.
- It's easy and cheap to travel around the country by bus or train, and there's now a fast train from Seoul to Pusan. For accommodation, *yogwan* are reliable and reasonably priced.
- Don't write a Korean name in red – it means the person is dead.
- Respect those older than you or in a position of authority.

- If someone offers you an empty glass, you hold it out towards them while they fill it with beer or soju. When pouring for someone else, it's polite to cup your left hand under your pouring (right) arm. Cheers is *kombeh!*
- Don't forget, kimchi is a good cure for a soju hangover!
- If you are working in South Korea, it's a very good idea to learn the intricacies of social customs. But if you're simply travelling around, people won't expect you to know everything – just observe what others are doing and be polite.
- Check with your local embassy to find out if you require a visa to enter South Korea.

CLIMATE

Spring: March to May (mild temperatures, spring flowers blossom)
Summer: June to August (rainy, hot, humid)
Autumn: September and October (mild temperatures, leaves change colour)
Winter: November to March (cold, snow)

KOREAN DISHES TO TRY

Bibimbap – rice with vegetables and fried egg, sometimes also beef

Dolsot bibimbap – as above but served in a hot earthenware bowl so it continues to cook

Bibim naengmyun – noodles with vegetables and hot sauce

Bulgogi – beef marinated in rice wine and sugar, served with rice

Kimchi tchigae – kimchi stew with tofu, sometimes also pork, served with rice and usually very hot and spicy

Kimbap – snack sushi, made with cooked ingredients, not raw fish

Mool naengmyun – cold noodles, broth, scissors – only for the adventurous

NOTE ON LANGUAGE – ALTERNATIVE SPELLINGS

A new official way of transcribing Korean words into English was introduced by the Ministry of Culture and Tourism in 2001. It is supposed to make it easier, but it doesn't help much with pronunciation, and differs confusingly from the old system. Generally K has become G (but Kim is still Kim!), Ch has become J, P has become B. Here are some common words and well-known places whose spelling has changed.

Changdokkung = Changdeokgung
Chindo = Jindo
Chongmyo = Jongmyo
Choson = Joseon (and is often called Yi)

hangul = hangeul
kimchi = gimchi
Koguryo = Goguryeo
Kongju = Gongju
Koryo = Goryeo
Kupabal = Gupabal
Kwanghwamun = Gwanghwamun
Kyungbokkung = Gyeongbokgung
Kyungju = Gyeongju
Myung-dong = Myeong-dong
Paekche = Baekje
Popchusa = Beopjusa
Pukansan = Bukhansan
Pyonsan = Byeonsan
Samgakchi = Samgakji
sam-ship = sam-sip
Shilla = Silla
Toksan = Deoksan

SELECT BIBLIOGRAPHY AND
USEFUL RESOURCES

Details correct at time of going to press.

A History of Modern Japan, Richard Storry (1960)
A Short History of Asia, Colin Mason (2005)
Building Peace and Democracy, Kim Dae-jung (1987)
Corea or Cho-sen, A. Henry Savage Landor (1895)
Find the Treasure Within, Seon Master Daehaeng
House of the Winds, Mia Yun (1998)
Korea: A Walk Through the Land of Miracles, Simon Winchester
(1988, reprinted 2004)
Korea's Place in the Sun, Bruce Cumings (1997)
Ten Thousand Sorrows, Elizabeth Kim (2000)
The Aquariums of Pyongyang, Kang Chol-hwan (2000)
The Korean War, editor David Rees (1984)
The Lonely Planet Guide to Korea
The Red Queen, Margaret Drabble (2004)
*Wake Up and Laugh: Dharma Talks by Korean Seon Master
Daehaeng* (2005)

www.koreanbook.de
www.hendrick-hamel.henny-savenije.pe.kr
www.seoulsearching.com
http://english.tour2korea.com/index.asp

http://www.koreaherald.co.kr
Jimoondang International Books in Korean Studies
(Edison, NJ)

Korean Cultural Centre
1 Northumberland Avenue, London WC2N 5EJ
0207 004 2600
www.london.korean-culture.org
Exciting art exhibitions, Korean film nights and a reference
library of books and electronic media, open to the public in
central London just off Trafalgar Square.

London Korean Links
www.londonkoreanlinks.net
Independent blog and resource centre for all things Korea-
related in the UK.

The Anglo-Korean Society
Regular events throughout the year, usually posted on
London Korean Links.

The East
The East Asian Monthly Business Newspaper
Free newspaper in English, found in Korean restaurants
across London. Very entertaining website.
www.theeast.org

Embassy of the Republic of Korea
60 Buckingham Gate
London SW1E 6AJ
0207 227 5500

British Korean Veterans Association
http://www.bkva.co.uk/

Korea Tourism Organization
www.visitkorea.or.kr

Cultural Heritage Administration
http://english.cha.go.kr/

Korean Culture and Information Service
www.korea.net

Seoul Metropolitan Government information site
http://english.seoul.go.kr/

Unimaster Travel
Flights to Korea
www.unimaster-travel.com

KOREAN FOOD I CAN RECOMMEND IN CENTRAL LONDON:

Asadal
227 High Holborn (next to Holborn tube station)
0207 430 9006
Hard to tell from outside but downstairs it's a spacious, upmarket restaurant with reasonable prices.

Bibimbab Café
37 Museum Street
0207 404 8880
Small café near the British Museum, limited menu but friendly!

Bi Won
24 Coptic Street
0207 580 2660
Small restaurant near the British Museum.

New Seoul
164 Clerkenwell Road
0871 332 7218
Very popular spot.

Woo Jung
59 St Giles High Street
0207 836 3103
Authentic, cheap and cheerful, just behind Centrepoint at Tottenham Court Road tube station. Afterwards you can pop into the Seoul Bakery for something sweet, then cross the road to stock up on supplies at...

Centre Point Food Store
20-21 St Giles High Street
Korean and Japanese food supplies.

To find a range of Korean restaurants and shops in one place, go to New Malden, south-west London. There's a range of excellent, authentic restaurants, but worth a trip for the decor alone is:

Han bar and restaurant
1 High Street
0208 949 7730
Spread over three floors, with sumptuously decorated raised private eating areas, water features and themed *norae-bang* (*karaoke* rooms).

ACKNOWLEDGEMENTS

A big thank you first of all to Gavin Mills, who not only invited me to South Korea but saw this book grow.

Warmest thanks also to Michael Bollen and Alastair Williams for agreeing to publish the book, to authors Margaret Drabble, Anna Nicholas and most of all Simon Winchester for generously giving your time and encouragement, and to Andy Davies for the beautiful cover design.

To everyone at Summersdale Publishers including Nicky Douglas, Elly Donovan, Dean Chant, Lucy York, Anna Martin, Stewart Ferris, Rob Smith and Bert Melhuish, and at Wakefield Press including Kathy Sharrad, Stephanie Johnston and Angela Tolley, and to Adrian Watson – thank you so much for your support and for being great to work with.

For valuable feedback and advice along the way, thanks to Will Aitken, Nicola Barr, Arjun Basu, Jane Boyd, Sarah Herman, Tatiana Wilde and Rebecca Winfield. If there's anyone I've omitted to mention, I apologise.

For introducing me to the Korean community in London, thanks to Soo Kim and most of all the tireless Philip Gowman.

Thanks as always to Mum, Peter and Dad, and to Duncan for issuing the challenge that it was too late for me to be a travel writer. And thank you to RW.

To Kim Wook-hyuon and all the other people who welcomed me to South Korea – this book is, of course, dedicated to you, and to peace and happy memories in Korea.

BUTTERTEA
AT SUNRISE

A Year in the Bhutan Himalaya

'A rare insight into life in this remarkable country'
Alec Le Sueur

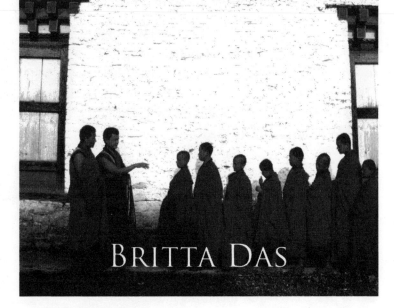

BRITTA DAS

Buttertea at Sunrise
A Year in the Bhutan Himalaya
Britta Das

ISBN 13: 978-1-84024-498-4 Paperback £7.99

Often seen as a magical paradise at the end of the world, Bhutan is inaccessible to most travellers. Set against the dramatic scenery of the Himalaya, this beautiful memoir reveals hardships and happiness in a land almost untouched by the West.

When Britta goes to work as a physiotherapist in a remote village hospital, her good intentions are put to the test amid monsoons, fleas and shocking conditions. But as she visits homes in the mountains and learns the mysteries of tantric Buddhism, the country casts its enduring spell.

Gaining insights into the traditions of this mystical kingdom, she makes friends and falls in love. Bhutan will change her life forever.

'a very interesting read beautifully written'

David Young, VSO

'Through the eyes of Britta Das, we gain valuable insight into the mysterious realm of Bhutan… compelling reading'

Michael Buckley, author of *Heartlands: Travels in the Tibetan World*

SINGAPORE SWING

JOHN MALATHRONAS

Singapore Swing

John Malathronas

ISBN 13: 978-1-84024-594-3 Paperback £7.99

For generations of Britons, Singapore was the international cross-roads of the Empire, the ultimate colonial posting, the stimulus for writers such as Joseph Conrad, Somerset Maugham and Noël Coward. Can today's high-tech 24-hour city with its gleaming skyscrapers and high standard of living provide a similar kind of inspiration to a visitor?

With fond memories of his time there as a backpacker, John Malathronas returns to Singapore to penetrate the oriental psyche and discovers the hustle among the stuffiness, the thrill behind the Confucian ethic and, ultimately, the *joie de vivre* in what has been unjustly dismissed as 'a shopping mall with UN representation'. Still more importantly, during his quest, spanning two trips, he realises that this overcrowded, multicultural, multifaith city-state can teach us a lesson about living together in harmony and with mutual respect.

John Malathronas is the author of the popular travelogues *Brazil: Life, Blood, Soul* and *Rainbow Diary: A Journey in the New South Africa*. He lives in London and is a member of the Guild of Travel Writers, contributing to magazines such as *Travel Africa*.

'… *a wealth of intriguing characters… an enjoyable book*'
                                                    REAL TRAVEL magazine

WWW.SUMMERSDALE.COM